*To Ling – gone but never forgotten.*
*Every time the sky looks magical – like the neons of*
*orange sunset, or a giant glowing moon – I think of you.*

this book belongs to

. . . . . . . . . . . . . . . . . . . . . . . . . . . . . . . . . . . .

Illustrated by
Aurelia Lange

# OPEN

# YOUR HEART
# LEARN TO LOVE
# YOUR LIFE AND
# LOVE YOURSELF
# GEMMA CAIRNEY
# WITH HELP FROM THE EXPERTS

**MACMILLAN**

First published 2017 as part of *Open: A Toolkit for How Magic and Messed Up Life Can Be*
by Macmillan Children's Books

This edition published 2018 by Macmillan Children's Books
an imprint of Pan Macmillan
20 New Wharf Road, London N1 9RR
Associated companies throughout the world
www.panmacmillan.com

ISBN 978-1-5098-7699-0

1 3 5 7 9 8 6 4 2

A CIP catalogue record for this book is available from
the British Library.

Designed by Janene Spencer
Printed and bound in China

# CONTENTS

I am brave
I am brash
I am bold
I am wild
I love to cuddle
I am loud . . . but
I am vulnerable
I love to smooch
I am serene
I am bored
BUT ALWAYS EXCITED
I am goofy
I am beautiful
Why do I find it so hard to write that?
I am deeply saddened
but at the same time so happy
I LOVE my life and I love the world
I sometimes don't like myself though
I am not perfect
I'm sometimes tired
I am always raring to go

I am as deep as an old well
I am shallow like a lame puddle
I am strange
which means I am normal
I am not preaching
I am a friend
with an OPEN heart

I am me.

# WELCOME

Welcome to *Open Your Heart: Learn to Love Your Life and Love Yourself.*

This book is here to be your guide in times of need. Keep it on your shelf and go to specific chapters during those moments in life that mess with your head, or leaf through and devour it cover to cover. By opening this book you have become part of #TeamOpen, and part of the movement for open hearts and minds. There is no one that this book isn't for.

During years of presenting, and more recently with *The Surgery* on BBC Radio 1, I've encountered a huge variety of people who are dealing with lots of different things in their own ways. My own life hasn't always been easy, and whilst I've dealt with some of the stuff that comes up in this book, I'm not an expert in everything – all I can do is communicate openly about what I've been through and be a friend. I've consulted lots of people who are experts in the issues covered, though – along with a list of people and organizations to speak to if you need more information on anything.

This book covers some tough stuff, but there's nothing you wouldn't find in the storyline of a popular soap opera, and definitely NOTHING you wouldn't find within a four-second Google search. *Open Your Heart* is about real life and everything that comes with it.

This book isn't all about me, it's also about you and all the other incredibly clever, brutally honest, brave and awesomely inspiring voices woven within its pages. This book is yours and I want you to personalize it in any way you see fit; to embellish it and make your own mark on the pages. There are no rules. Douse it in gorgeous gold pen, doodle across it with a blunt pencil or a defiant marker pen, or cover it in magical stickers – and whatever your approach, feel free to respond to however the words make you feel.

 Just 🐝 You

# DEAR READER

It's only been a year since the original *Open* was written, my blood, guts and pumping heart stitched together in a book – and SO much has happened since then. Time is an oddity when it comes to love and fun. It moves slowly on halcyon days, new surroundings and hazy holidays, or when you're waiting for the clock to move quicker and are looking forward to seeing someone or doing something in the future. But time, when it comes to love, can flip fast too. I look back breathlessly at this year and realize that love can change as intensely as it's created. Love is a storm, a perfect one – crashing, loud, wet, intense, exciting and scary.

## Love, love, and all those fish in the sea

Have you ever opened your eyes underwater when swimming without goggles or a diving mask on? Exposed your eyeballs to the mystic scene underwater? Experienced the sparkling swimming-pool blues or those shafts of light that sear through the sea from the sun? It's beautiful. There's a second, maybe two, a few beats where everything feels magic. Then you realize you can't breathe, and that the loveliness has ended as quickly as it began. So you charge upwards to reach the surface again, to grab some necessary air. Once you're back in the air, you breathe for a while, take in what happened down there and bob along the top, kicking your feet, treading water as you go. Love feels like this for me right now. I've experienced yet another heartbreak since writing *Open*. Not only that, but I've cried out old ones too. I'm soaked in all the emotions of break-up and overblown thought and excitement for new horizons, bobbing along on the top, trying to catch a breath, still treading water. Trying to avoid jellyfish of the stinging variety – jellyfish called regret, bitterness, stupid decisions and societal expectation, I'm doggy-paddling to somewhere, where there are lots of tropical and lovely fish. There are plenty of fish in this sea.

I've even found myself reading the Heartbreak chapter of my own book, remembering that this thing called heartbreak, though it can ache, will get better. And at the end of the day, when I was putting my heart on the weighing scales, weighing up being either alone and happy or with someone and sad, I knew I had to take my own advice.

# A Volcano family

I'm not sure how I expected to get away with writing about the importance of 'opening up' without some of my bloodlines and relations doing the same. It's been a heady process – my own family members reaching out to tell me stories, and have important conversations and a bit of emotional grappling. But overall it's been important. I stand by the fact that life's a journey – there isn't one day when everything makes sense and you are protected from how family can bring up ALL THE FEELS. Everything written about my family is only my opinion after all. We all experience life in different ways and nobody is one thing, or one person's experience of them. I've learned to remember that it is never too late to reconnect with those in your family who once upset you or let you down, and to always assess whether raw emotion blurs solutions which might be better in the long run.

We can be whoever we damn well want to be, do whatever we want and change our own mind on whatever we fancy. There ain't nothing set in stone when it comes to our hearts, minds and decisions – not even loved ones.

# Naked truth

This summer I took part in an experiment for BBC Radio 4's *Woman's Hour*, with the brief to do less doom-mongering 'stats-based studio chat' and more actual ACTION: to get out there and talk to people on the streets. Two other presenters and I were given three days to come up with an activity or product that made women feel better about their bodies. I learned about the powerful feeling known as 'embodiment' from an expert psychologist specializing in body image.

There is a theory that in order to experience a positive understanding of our body, we need first and foremost to grasp and accept its importance in keeping us alive. My journey to capture this feeling has been both empowering and fun: I learned about the brilliance of life drawing by posing nude for a charcoal-sketching artist. Don't get me wrong, it was mightily strange pulling down my pants in front of my radio producer (I was hoping for a glamorous robe) but I kept on my Converse for good measure! It was fun not to be naked for washing or sex but just to sit with my naked self and let someone get lost in the shapes it forms by simply drawing it. We're so embarrassed by nudity in our culture and society – but I think there could be something in the idea of letting that go.

Just when you think you know everything about loving your life, your friends, your body and yourself, you'll learn a whole heap more. If there's something I'm sure of, it's that I'll never stop learning and I'll never stop loving.

This book is about every kind of love and relationship that might come your way, and what to do when it does.

Gemma

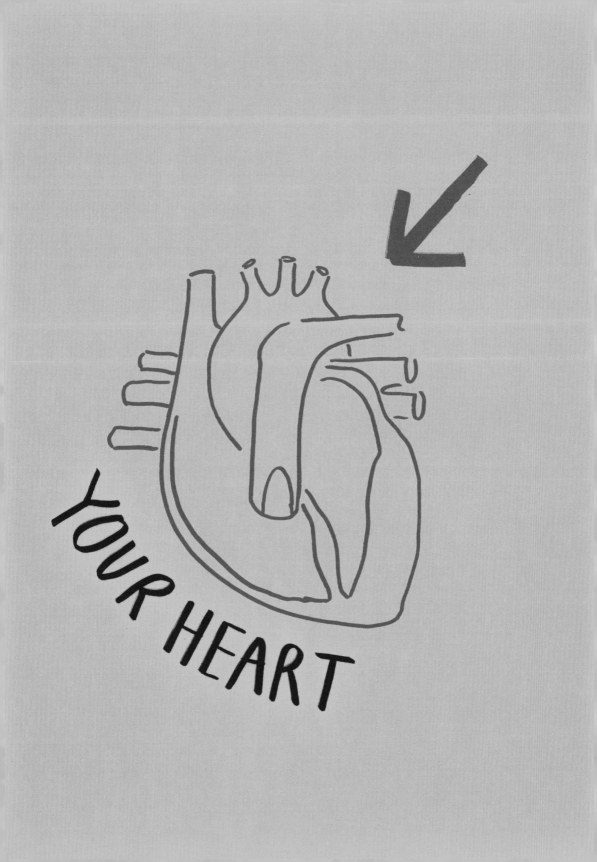

 is precious. It is AWESOME. Not only does it pump blood around your body to keep you alive, but it is the root of your deepest emotions.

 is your Emotional Mothership, your inner hub – the place where you feel joy, happiness, anger, fear, sadness, heartbreak, confusion – a cosmic, blinding mass of feelings that can sometimes feel overwhelming but make you the unique and incredible human being that you are.

 is tough – it is a warrior – it will heal you and bring you joy as much as it will cause you to hurt and even to physically ache sometimes. Right now I'm taking you on a journey through your heart, through the people and situations that touch your heart, that bump it along the way, that soothe it and that make it want to burst with emotions.

REMEMBER that at the centre of your heart is a wonderful, scary, intangible and dizzyingly powerful thing called **LOVE**.

Love is your greatest ally. Whether it is for people, music, plants — or a goldfish, LOVE ALWAYS WINS.

# FAMILY

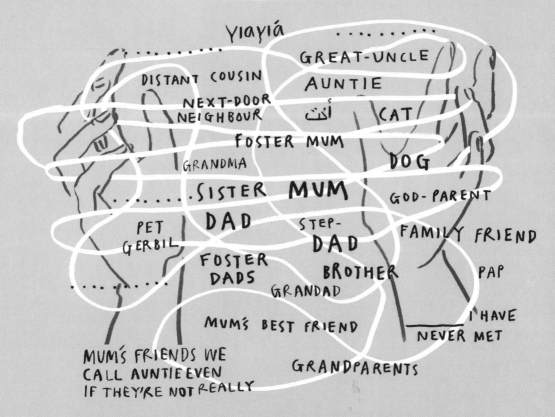

γιαγιά
GREAT-UNCLE
DISTANT COUSIN
AUNTIE
NEXT-DOOR
NEIGHBOUR
أختي
CAT
FOSTER MUM
GRANDMA
DOG
SISTER MUM
GOD-PARENT
PET GERBIL
DAD
STEP-
DAD
FAMILY FRIEND
FOSTER DADS
BROTHER
PAP
GRANDAD
I HAVE
NEVER MET
MUM'S BEST FRIEND
MUM'S FRIENDS WE
CALL AUNTIE EVEN
IF THEY'RE NOT REALLY
GRANDPARENTS

Families are like balls made up of elastic bands, wrapped and bound and wound around each other, linked by similarities and connections. We are linked to others, but individuals too. The truth is that families aren't perfect, ever. More often than not, families are far from 'conventional'. But these peeps, the ones who brought us into the world, help form who we are and who we will go on to be.

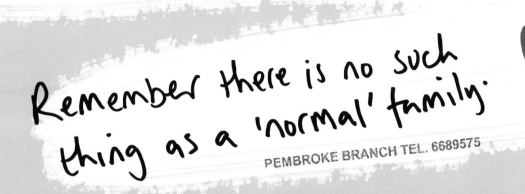

Remember there is no such thing as a 'normal' family.

PEMBROKE BRANCH TEL. 6689575

Let's kick off with PARENTS. When it comes to parents, we love to label them, don't we? There are step-parents, divorced parents, single parents, adopted parents, foster parents, estranged parents, good parents, bad parents, boring parents, uptight parents, possessive parents, depressed parents, parents that argue, so-in-love-it-grosses-us-out-cos-we-hear-them-having-sex-sometimes parents, parents-we-never-see-for-some-reason-like-'they-are-always-at-work' parents, parents who are hard to please, parents who have passed away, parents we miss so much it makes our eyes sting at the thought of them.

Then there are those beings (more like aliens) we call siblings: BROTHERS and SISTERS. When it comes to brothers and sisters, the labels and emotive descriptions come thick and fast out of the box again: step-siblings, siblings you get on really well with, siblings you hate, siblings you envy, competitive siblings, siblings you have nothing to say to, siblings you've never met, half-brothers or half-sisters.

Or of course you might be an ONLY CHILD, or maybe you feel like an only child because your sibling or siblings are a lot older or younger than you and you didn't grow up with them.

## IT'S COMPLICATED...

Hand in the air if you can identify with one or more of these families? Millions of us have higgledy-piggledy, eclectic family trees. Some of us have detailed horror stories and fabulous family-specific tales that drip from the leaves too. I do, and so do most of the people I know. Even if we find our personal family patchwork generally OK, at some point EVERYONE FINDS THEIR FAMILY EMBARRASSING. No one – and I repeat NO ONE – escapes that.

# chatting to your 'rents

When the poo hits the fan, hopefully you can talk to your mum or dad, or your foster parent, or your guardian – whoever looks after you – about your worries and fears. If you don't feel like you have someone who fits that description, then find someone who is older than you, wiser than you, that you trust and who gives good advice. Even if that person is on the end of a phone. These people do exist, I promise. A teacher, a doctor or someone from a qualified organization or support network – if life is getting tough, they'll help you start to figure out what is puzzling you or bringing you down. Even if they can't perform perfect wizardry and magic answers out of the air, they will be able to point you in the right direction.

**A problem shared can be a problem halved.**

# College / university

Research what help is available to you here, even if you're not feeling like you need help right now – it's good to know that it's there for you. Most colleges and universities provide free and confidential in-house counselling services, with professionally qualified counsellors and access to specific external advice.

# Teacher / school

Schools are set up and ready to hear from their students, whether it's about exam pressure or problems at home.

# Your Workplace

Many companies have an HR department. The HR stands for Human Resources and is designed to protect the well-being of the employee, especially if it is an issue relating to the workplace itself. Some HR departments are better than others (they aren't always the answer). But it's worth researching yours specifically and knowing your rights within your place of work. Ask around and work out what's in place to protect and look after you.

# A mate's mum

Sometimes borrowing someone else's mum is pretty helpful. They can offer an unbiased perspective as well as having the mum qualities you need.

# Your GP/ doctor

If you break your arm, you go to the doctor. If you are feeling stressed, anxious and filled with heartache because of it, your doctor may be able to help with this too.

## When your parents are being hot-headed monsters and saying no to something . . .

When you feel that parents are acting all unapproachable and saying no to something you want to do, remember that most of them instinctively want to protect you, feed you and get you educated and equipped. They want to prepare you for the big wide world. They literally can't help it. Imagine if you could see your face in someone smaller than you, and that you've been through life's highs and lows, and all you want more than anything in the whole wide world is for the face of the person smaller than you to be smiling and oozing joy. You'd WRESTLE A DINOSAUR to protect them.

Even though families can make us roar like no other and prod our emotional pressure points in a way that only they can, I want you to know that your family is only doing its job, which is to make you generally feel loved and safe. If you are reading this with a family member nearby, go give them a cuddle. Or do it next time you see them. Then answer this:

### Did it make you glow and feel warm inside?

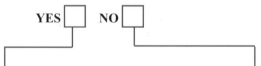

YES ☐    NO ☐

**If the answer is YES** to feeling warm and glowing from the inside from hugging at least one of your family members, then this a good sign – remember this next time you feel like they are against you!

**If the answer is NO** and you are not getting on with any of your family, you are lacking their presence in any way, you feel truly alone or in your gut you are very uncomfortable with something that's going on in your family at the moment – please read on.

# DYSFUNCTIONAL FAMILIES

There is a difference between a MESSY family and a family that makes you feel unsafe or uncared for. Hopefully you have someone in your family who is strong and looks out for you – but issues such as alcoholism, addiction, depression, divorce, money worries or unemployment can rock your parents and make it difficult for them to cope. Please remember it is not your job to take on their problems, but there are people you can talk to about how to cope with your own feelings.

## Please ask yourself these three things:

1) **Is it affecting your everyday life?** ☐
2) **Are you scared in any way?** ☐
3) **Would you like some extra help with this situation?** ☐

If you ticked any of the above, please tell someone in authority that you are feeling this way and why. I REPEAT: speak to a teacher, or your GP, if that seems more appropriate, or head to the back of this book for a list of organizations that are expert in helping with specific issues, no matter how hard or scary they seem. You are NOT alone.

Who's your Daddy?

I'm going to tell you my story...

From the age of seven, like many kids I knew, I grew up in a single-parent household. It was my mum who brought me and my sister up, though we'd see our dad regularly – a man I wholly adore.

My dad is a gentle, lovely, sweet, friendly man – he moved to the UK from Jamaica when he was eight, and his face is the kindest I've ever seen. In the late 1970s he used to be the guitarist in a band called the High Flames, a fact I will never not find brilliantly glamorous. He still plays guitar, and can copy any tune from an advert and transform it into funk. His favourite band is Earth, Wind & Fire – one of the grooviest bands your ears could hear.

On my dad's fiftieth birthday it seemed like the whole of his estate came to the birthday barbecue, because everyone loves him. They practically lined up to tell me how cool they thought he was. The grannies enthused about how they could moan till they were blue in the face to him and he would always listen, how they loved that he'd still go to church every Sunday and

genuinely cared if they were OK. Even the naughtiest-of-naughty bad boys on the estate loved him. I think it's because he never judges, he cares passionately about social justice, thinks anything is possible, and his resting face is the warmest smile! If the sun had a face, it'd smile like my dad's. He always looks cool too – ironed short-sleeved shirt, slick, gelled curls, sparklingly clean sunglasses and a heavy, dependable watch. He's a hero. He and my mum didn't work out, but that's their stuff. I'm eternally lucky to have him in my life.

One of the most amazing things about my dad is that he is not my 'biological' dad, my 'real' dad. I never knew my real dad (I don't like that phrase, 'real dad' – it doesn't describe what feels 'real' to me in relation to how I feel about either of my dads. The most I knew about my biological dad – my BD – is that he was a wildly charismatic, deep-voiced firework of a man, who had a gold tooth. He had Jamaican parents too, was from the Midlands, loved to party, was sometimes violent and was an alcoholic.

When I was nineteen, I got a letter from the Samaritans, who informed me that they'd had an enquiry from a distant family member of mine who would like to get in touch. I knew instantly it would have something to do with this other dad of mine, floating out there somewhere. A dad for whom I'd never felt the need, because I already had one, who was the grooviest, smiliest, funniest dad of all dads.

Out of intrigue, I agreed to be put in contact with whoever it was that had enquired. It turned out to be the sister of my BD – an aunt I'd never met – and she wanted to tell me that he'd died. I'd never known this man, but a spiral of mashed feelings washed over me, as if someone had turned out the lights and put on a continuous flickering strobe instead. It didn't feel like direct and identifiable grief – it felt more like when you hear about someone dying that you may have only met once. It made me sad, but it didn't make me want to fall to the ground and smash everything up. I hadn't seen this man since I was three – he hadn't been part of my life. I didn't know what I felt. I almost couldn't feel.

Around this time, I met with my 'real' grandparents – one of the most startling experiences of my life, seeing my own face in these two people's faces. It was frankly insane. But then I decided to move on. I got on with my early twenties, carried on disco-dancing, smooching hotness and chasing dreams. But grief got to me all the same. Even though I didn't recognize it. It began gnawing at my insides, sometimes in the form of a searing pain in my chest. It was a longing for answers, a buried anxiety about the alcoholism that had killed this stranger who was my dad. My feelings were chewed up – sometimes making me self-destructive.

Eventually I worked through these feelings and threw myself into life, with the one thing that I was wholly sure of strapped to my back: that I LOVE LIFE. But what I learned was that grief – especially when it's for family – can flip open your heart, and out come unexpected messy feelings and pain you aren't prepared for. I realized that even though he wasn't around for me, my BD is still part of me, part of my identity, and I tortured myself thinking about his drinking, wondering if anyone could have stopped him. But his addiction wasn't my fault – I had to learn that. Even though it affected me more than I realized.

I worked on my 'happy' – surrounded myself with things and people that made me glow inside. Dug deep to face up to the sad and confusing stuff in my heart and turn it into energy – to charge forward and be brave.

And now? Now I don't question what I should feel about either of my Jamaican dads: my BD, who I never knew and whose face I've inherited, and the one who is still here for me, whose face is like the sunshine and the kindest and most dignified man I've been lucky enough to know. I feel OK. I love and am proud to have my heart beating to a reggae rhythm, and to have a soul that now understands how complicated families can be.

Everyone has a family tale to tell.

### Lauren, from Garmouth, Scotland

Lauren's mum and dad split up when she was six. After that, she says, her dad 'gradually lost touch' with her and her sister. Her mum has since remarried, and her stepdad has adopted her. Lauren says, 'Last time I spoke to my biological dad, he was working for Virgin trains – so every time I use one I wonder if he's driving.'

### Michael, from Scarborough

'I have three mums and three dads – the perks of being adopted and having step-parents also. I'm in contact with every single one of them too. My mum and dad will always be my parents, but I'm grateful to my birth mum, for her sacrifice to give me the best possible upbringing.'

### Sophie, from Sussex

'Having a gay dad and a gay brother is something I am so proud of. It represents the diversity and acceptance in my family; it demonstrates an unconditional love we all have for each other; but most of all it makes me happy that they are content to be themselves. It is very special and is at the heart of what makes my unconventional family truly awesome.'

# FAMILY BINGO

Roll up, roll up. Who's for a game of FAMILY BINGO?
Simply fill in the blanks: write the thing you most like
and dislike about all the flavours of your family.

| Name: | Name: | Name: | Name: | Name: |
|---|---|---|---|---|
| Good: | Good: | Good: | Good: | Good: |
| Bad: | Bad: | Bad: | Bad: | Bad: |
| Name: | Name: | Name: | Name: | Name: |
| Good: | Good: | Good: | Good: | Good: |
| Bad: | Bad: | Bad: | Bad: | Bad: |
| Name: | Name: | **ME** | Name: | Name: |
| Good: | Good: | | Good: | Good: |
| Bad: | Bad: | | Bad: | Bad: |
| Name: | Name: | Name: | Name: | Name: |
| Good: | Good: | Good: | Good: | Good: |
| Bad: | Bad: | Bad: | Bad: | Bad: |
| Name: | Name: | Name: | Name: | Name: |
| Good: | Good: | Good: | Good: | Good: |
| Bad: | Bad: | Bad: | Bad: | Bad: |

Draw a line from the ME box to all the things you think you've
inherited from your family – good or bad. You might find
you've got more in common than you think.

# READING, LISTENING & WATCHING LIST ON FAMILY

## Watching

**Television series and films**

*The Royle Family*
*Gilmore Girls*
*Brothers & Sisters*
*The Goldbergs*
*The Royal Tenenbaums*
*Raised by Wolves*
*Little Miss Sunshine*

## Reading

*The Catcher in the Rye* – J. D. Salinger
*I Capture the Castle* – Dodie Smith
*Red Ink* – Julie Mayhew
*Paper Aeroplanes* – Dawn O'Porter
*Little Women* – Louisa May Alcott

## Listening

'We Are Family' – The Pointer Sisters
'Everybody's Free' – Quindon Tarver
'When Doves Cry' – Prince
'Sweet Mother' – Skepta
'It's a Family Affair' – Sly and the Family Stone

# FRIENDSHIP

I am a map of my friends. A big tangled map of roads, paths, avenues, forests, woods and rivers, each representing the people I love in my life. No one else can make me feel as raucous or as safe, as defiant or as carefree and fun. No one else has the ability to yank me out when I am stuck in a patch of quicksand sadness.

With our friends we are our nuanced* and evolving selves. No matter how large or small your crew of mates is, at any one time

chips are down, who make you laugh and let you cry. A good friend is someone who won't just tell you what you want to hear, but that you can trust not to bullshit you. A good friend knows that you have boundaries and won't cross them.

Imagine you are a bonfire. You need the right wood as your foundation. The bad, rotten, wrong type of wood won't help your flame roar bright. I am in awe of the magic humans I've encountered who keep

# YOU'VE GOT A FRIEND

in your life, they are a fragmented mosaic of personality-filled mirrors, reflecting how you want to treat yourself at that time. Different groups of friends make up the chapters to your internal book. They can challenge you if you are being reckless, and they can help you take risks when you need to.

The saying 'choose your friends wisely' is true. Good friends are those who don't pressure or manipulate you, who cheer when you're doing well, and hug you when the

my bonfire alight. My friends make me feel good about who I am most of the time, and it's one of life's biggest pleasures if I can reciprocate that, and help them feel the same.

I hope you are reading this, nodding and feeling the same way too. Think of the people out of all those you call friends that just rock! They sparkle! They are fantastic! Think about the remarkable memories you've made together. Feel proud, as it is a reflection of how fantastic you must be too.

*'Nuance' is one of my favourite words. Here's its definition, in case ya didn't already have its meaning under your belt:
**Nuance:** a subtle difference in or shade of meaning, expression or sound.

Who are your friends? Write their names here:

# FANTASTIC FRIENDSHIPS

*Word wall, built with a little help from my friends...*

MISCHIEF
LAUGHTER HONESTY
MUTUAL RESPECT
EASE
FUN
TRUTH FORGIVENESS
COMMUNICATION
COMFORTABILITY COMFORT
LOYALTY

# A TRUE MATE WILL ALWAYS HAVE YOUR BACK

Once, with one of my best friends – Bri – I gave a talk on the importance of female friendship throughout history. As we started to scratch the surface, we were shocked to find that there aren't many examples that have been documented. There were a couple of examples that I found to be pretty cool, though – as follows:

# Anne Bonny and Mary Read

Described as 'fierce hellcats' – Anne Bonny and Mary Read were swashbuckling, filthy, dangerous and rare female pirates in the1700s. Instantly thick as thieves in 1720, when their unbreakable friendship was formed, they set sail the same year on a ship called *Revenge*. Anne was outwardly female, while Mary had had a history of keeping her born gender under wraps, and had joined the military years previously under the name of Mark, dressed as a man. Anne kept Mary's secret for as long as she could (some stories say a romance developed between the pair). That was until Anne's husband, Calico Jack – who was also a pirate on the ship – became too jealous of his wife flirting with 'Mark' onboard.

Anne and Mary's friendship saw them through the rough piracy and crime-filled seas of the West Indies for a year. Together with the rest of the ship's crew they navigated rough seas, fought enemy ships and drank together. In 1721, the ship was finally caught – and all on board were tried for the crime of piracy and were hanged. All, that is, except for Mary and Anne, who both escaped the death sentence by 'pleading the belly' – otherwise known as declaring pregnancy. In jail they had adjoining cells to await the birth of their children. Sadly, Mary died of a ferocious fever before giving birth, while Anne's fate is unknown. BFFs till the bitter end.

B.F.F

# Marilyn Monroe and Ella Fitzgerald

A little-known and inspiring tale of female friendship that I stumbled across was that of Hollywood actress Marilyn Monroe and jazz musician Ella Fitzgerald. Back in 1950s America, racism was rife and segregation all too prevalent in many states. Ella, despite being hugely talented and popular, struggled to push through prejudice against the colour of her skin, and was banned from playing many live music venues, purely for being a black woman. A certain notorious club of the time, the Mocambo Nightclub in Los Angeles, was no exception.

Marilyn Monroe, a regular at the club, was so stirred and outraged on learning of Ella's treatment that she rang the owner of the Mocambo personally and demanded they hire Ella immediately, declaring that she, Marilyn, would sit at the front table every night Ella performed. At the time, Marilyn was one of the biggest movie stars on the planet, and she knew her presence would attract the kind of publicity that Mocambo couldn't resist. The club complied, and Marilyn made sure she was there, at the front table every single night that Ella performed. The press went bonkers, and as a result Ella Fitzgerald's success propelled to stratospheric heights. Marilyn and Ella remained good friends.

Friends come in all forms – and the good ones will always have your back, no matter what.

# Are you a good friend?

Ask your mates on WhatsApp now what it's like to be your friend! It's daunting, but illuminating. I just did, and I learned that I need to be better at answering my phone to some mates, but that some of my mates find me optimistic – which is nice.

What did you learn from asking your mates what kind of friend you are?

I'M A BIT OF A FLAKY FRIEND

Flake

# FRENEMIES

## The late friend

The one you harbour fairly deep annoyance about. You know that they aren't evil, so you can't not be their friend any more. You JUST DON'T understand how they can ALWAYS be THAT late.

LATE

(again!)

## The flaky friend

One step further along the toxic scale than the late friend is the FLAKY one. They are just NEVER there when you need them to be. You cannot understand how they always seem to be doing fun things on social media when they always have an excuse to cancel on you at the last minute.

## The competitive friend

The one that JUST has to have one up on you. They quash your good news with theirs. They are usually harbouring secret envy – a telltale sign for this being their bruised look every time you tell them about something awesome that has happened to you.

# WHO ARE THEY?

## The self-obsessed friend

The mate who you know full well you'll be acting as a therapist for whenever you see them. This mate is unlikely to ask you how you are EVER.

## The friend you don't trust

... with the one you fancy, because they will flirt with them. Also the one who you just know says one thing to one person, another to another, and so on. The friend with MANY faces.

## The toxic friend

This is the worst type. The toxic friend makes you feel bad about yourself, puts you down, lets you down, never has your back.

If any of your friends are in the pink zone, then TALK to them about how they make you feel. Chances are they have no idea how their behaviour is affecting you. If any of them are in the red zone, then consider unfriending them. Chances are they know what they are doing and won't change.

# BEING BULLIED

Bullying is universal, in schools, places of work, in relationships and online. It makes the bullied feel as small as a shirt button, as alone as a lost plastic bag bobbing around in the wind. It devastates your sense of security. It can make you feel like your world is caving in. It makes you feel powerless.

## IT SUCKS.
## YOU ARE WORTH MORE.

Bullies are essentially troubled individuals who lack self-esteem and draw their power from making other people feel worthless and small. They are often victims of bullying themselves, so they know how it works. Being bullied feels like you are drowning in irrational hostility and meanness. It can truly overshadow any positivity and joy you feel, and put you in a place where you actually believe that you deserve this treatment.

Don't let the harshness win. It isn't your problem, it's theirs. Remember that bullies are feeling their own pain too. Bullies are people who have not got to the bottom of their darkness. They don't like themselves, but are unable to face up to their problems. Their hearts are hurting too. OUCH. It hurts all round.

But here's the thing: YOU have power, more than you know. You can choose how bullying is dealt with. Switch off your phone, tell someone in authority, call someone out for being a bully. As a type of abuse, bullying is well acknowledged as deeply upsetting and is thankfully now taken very seriously. All bullying is wrong – there is a never a case where it's OK to bully. Things can get better if you try to protect yourself by finding the strength to walk away from this negative behaviour. Never suffer alone: TELL SOMEONE IMMEDIATELY.

If you are a bully, it's time to STOP and work out why you are doing it in the first place. What gives you the right to put someone through this hell? Being kind to people feels so much better.

There is some brilliant anti-bullying information and advice from anti-bullying ambassadors on www.antibullyingpro.com. Head there for more information.

If you'd like some extra help telling someone you are being bullied, please use the letter template below. Either photocopy it, fill in the blanks and post it through the appropriate person's door, or copy it into an email and send it to that person instead.

```
Dear . . .


I've been wanting to tell you that I'm being bullied and it's
starting to really get me down. I wanted to open up. It's been
quite hard to tell anyone because I'm (delete as applicable)
scared/embarrassed/afraid/ashamed/feeling very sad about it.

It is happening as regularly as . . . . . time(s) a week.

It is taking place in the form of (delete as applicable) online
bullying/face-to-face bullying.

Examples
below:.............................................................
..................................................................
..................................................................

I'd like to talk to you more about it.
Please call or email me back on...................................

Thank you. Your support on this would be so hugely appreciated.

From

..................................................................
```

# BREAKING UP
# WITH FRIENDS

The so-called friends who mostly make you feel ANGUISH and UNCERTAINTY, or have too often LED YOU ASTRAY, are usually better off as friends of the past rather than the present. It's not easy to distance yourself from certain people, but sometimes it's the best thing you can do to protect yourself and your peace of mind. You don't have to be unkind – just don't see them one-on-one any more – make sure it's in wider groups only, so that it's not so intense. Fill your time with activities that you love, and the mates that make you howl with laughter and make you feel good about yourself. You'll soon be 'too busy' to be sucked of energy by a manipulative, stinky bad egg.

# BE YOUR OWN
# BEST FRIEND

So we've established that your mates are very important. But the fact is that your friendship with YOURSELF is the most important one you'll ever have.

Be your own best friend. Be kind to yourself and take control of how your life plays out. Stop beating yourself up if you make a mistake – learn from mistakes; accept who you are and what makes you tick.

# DO THINGS THAT MAKE YOU FEEL GOOD IN YOUR OWN COMPANY:

* Take a dog for a walk
* Have a massage
* Head to the steam room of your local pool
* Try giving yourself a pedicure
* Go and take photos of beautiful things
* Smile at your reflection in the mirror

* Make a gigantic homemade pizza that has so many toppings it looks like a compost bin has exploded
* Knit or crochet a miniature scarf
* Watch a great box set
* Dance alone in your bedroom
* Jump on the bed

* Write – a book, a blog, a diary
* Draw, paint or colour something in
* Read
* Download and listen to an audio book
* Express yourself, however you can and however you want.

Learn self-reliance. It is ace and can help make you strong. It's a way to learn to trust your own instincts and take care of yourself – mind and body. Learning to like your own company and being fully independent is as GOOD for you as finding the love of your life.

Five things I like to do/would like to do by myself.

1)

2)

3)

4)

5)

# LOVE

Oh cripes. This stuff is the deepest of all.
It's the heavy stuff. But, oh my goodness . . .
When it's GOOD –

*it's gooood.*

# THE REAL THING

So, what about L.O.V.E.? I'm not talking about our obsession with thumping hearts on screens – I'm talking about the real stuff. The dizzying stuff. The stuff that can make you gulp, make your mouth dry up and your face crumple into a squishy, happy sad-clown face. The love that makes you cry and throb. The real love. The romantic type. The most-confusing-of-all type. An emoji just isn't going to work for this.

## The love letter to love

Dear Love,

I love you for always being there.

I love how you are only truly described through song and kisses.

Thank you for helping me to patch out some of my flaws and feel totally floored whilst doing it.

I've learned that in your maddest moments it can sometimes be impossible to speak, to think straight, to be afraid of anything, even death.

Thank you for making me understand what it's like to be an insane, raging beast.

Thanks for twisting my morals to help me define them.

Thank you for continuing to return. Even when I think you have gone for good.

Thank you for those moments, when I'm looking for the meaning of life, that I'm reminded it's you.

Love,
Gem

Your love is bespoke, and so is mine. It can mean a different thing to each of us. The reliability and security found in many partnerships is vital for some and not others. It's too easy to fall into a trap of looking around too much – to want to have what others have, purely out of pack mentality. It's important to swim in your own love channel and decide what's right for the rhythm of your own heartbeat.

REAL love can feel like being out of control, and you cannot necessarily always predict WHO you love and HOW you love. Sometimes you want to keep it casual – sometimes you don't. Sometimes the person you love will want something different from you. No best friend, family member or even book can tell you what to do when it comes to whether YOU should be attracted to someone, get together with someone, break up with someone, get back together with someone, or if you would be better off alone. Your love is your love, and you know it better than anyone. If you're feeling confused by who you love or worried about telling the people around you about them because you think they won't approve, then this is when it's most important to listen to your heart and be guided by it.

. . . No one tells you this, but strong and healthy relationships of all kinds need WORK. Just like plants need care and nurturing to grow. Unfortunately relationships don't come with instructions on how to maintain them – that's something you have to learn all by yourself.

# THE WALTZER

Love. Oh yes. It's like being on a waltzer at the funfair:
it's hard to focus, a bit sickening, exciting, thrilling and scary,
and you are definitely not alone if you are . . .

feeling a bit
obsessed with
someone right
now.

Keep
reading.

desperately
heartbroken and
think you will never be
the same again.

Head to page 42
on heartbreak
and what it can and
can't do.

in the wrong
relationship and
need to assess why and
how you might want
to get out.

Keep
reading.

# SPLITTING UP IS BORING

Whenever I've split up with someone, it's been because I start to get a headache. My head aches with keeping them happy and with trying to work out why they don't make me feel like myself any more, and it aches even more at the relentless thoughts of splitting up with them.

There is no easy way of splitting up with someone.

EVEN IF YOU CAN'T BE
BOTHERED WITH ALL THE
MESS THAT COMES WITH
BREAKING UP. EVEN THOUGH
YOU MIGHT EVEN STILL LOVE
THEM. I'M SORRY TO HAVE
TO TELL YOU THIS, BUT...
IF YOU WANT TO SPLIT
UP WITH SOMEBODY, THEN
YOU NEED TO DO IT.

Regardless of how much you adore that person's family, or remember the promises you once made to them, or the pet you share, or are worried what your bed will feel like without them in it.

**Be brave, rip the plaster off. It will be painful. But, once the rain has stopped, a rainbow may appear.**

# I'M NOT IN LOVE

**Love is fluid,** it changes all the time, and if you're lucky it just gets deeper. Some of us need to be 'in love' – we need fireworks and piping hot 'smoochy' times, like in romcoms and songs, or like our friends who seem to 'have it all'. If that doesn't happen straight away, then often we panic and think it can't be right.

**Calm down.** We have a lifetime to love, and love when it arrives can be beautifully unique, subtle and different from what you've known before. Being 'in love' with a person can happen after a while, when you've really got to know them. When that happens, it's amazing, because it is built on something real, and not just attraction, or brain-mangling infatuation. Attraction is very important, but that might happen later too. Someone can definitely become more attractive the more you know them.

**Take your time,** and don't rush or make rash decisions. You don't need to verbally commit to anything at all. Chill, sit in the park on a blanket together, get to know each other. You don't need to go running to Vegas to get married. Only do that if it's the real 'holy-moly' deal.

**Your life is not a film.**

MY LOVE ZONE

PSSSSSTTTT . . . At the time of writing, I have had five noteworthy partners and fallen in love six different times (two of those times were with the same person). The first time I fell in love I was twelve years old. But love is not about numbers – it's about people. If you were to see each of my loves in a line-up, you would be befuddled by what a hotchpotch you'd see.

I am open to all sorts, as long as I see a magic about them. I've had to learn the hard way about 'Love versus Madness'. Each of my loves impacted on me big. A couple of them impacted on me monstrously. Out of the five, two ended up being toxic for me (typically, I was madly in love with those people at the time). They were dangerous loves that eroded my well-being. (Please head to page 39 for more on abusive relationships.)

The other three are great people with kindness in their hearts who taught me that I am lovable and worthy of someone dreamy and amazing. I will always consider these three loves friends, even if I don't see some of them much any more. And the one I'm with now (who was actually my downstairs neighbour) is a really good one, thank goodness.

If there's one thing I've learned, it's that you never know who you're going to meet, or who you'll fall for in this life, or how it will happen. And that, my friend, is EXCITING.

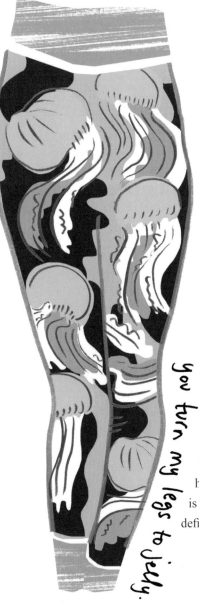

you turn my legs to jelly.

# INFATUATION

Once I was so infatuated with a boy it was painful. I just couldn't wash him out of my hair. I'd think about him all the time. I'd carefully plan what I was going to wear the next time I saw him. Whenever we were near one another, I felt the kind of electric bolts through my body that could create power cuts. I couldn't take my eyes off him in a crowd . . . He drove me crazy. It wasn't exactly fun.

Sometimes this boy chose to talk to me at the end of the night, or to kiss me. Sometimes he didn't. Sometimes he'd choose somebody else to wrap himself around instead. It hurt, but it also made him more intoxicating. He was charismatic, vulnerable and a little mean, but he never failed to make me erupt with laughter.

I talked about this boy a LOT, trying to work out whether he felt the same. In the end a friend of mine got so bored with my infatuation that one day she opened up her computer and played the new song she'd written. It is called 'Dickhead' and is by Kate Nash and you should definitely give it a listen.

# The side-effects of
# REJECTION

Most of us have been rejected. It is never pleasant. Often, splitting up is not a mutual decision and, if you are the one being 'rejected' or dumped, hopefully it will be done as kindly as possible, so you're not left in a mess. But then there are those who keep you dangling and insecure and never properly commit, only to reject you in the end. If you are chasing after someone who's not totally interested in you, it can seriously rattle your self-esteem. You don't always realize how it is making you feel about yourself at the time, but to be aware of the side-effects of rejection can be helpful and will stop you from beating yourself up about it.

Days or months later, even when you've moved on from that particular person, you may find yourself feeling that you are not attractive or interesting enough, that there's something wrong with you. There is nothing wrong with you, except for the fact that you once tried to love someone who didn't love you back. Your pride took such a hit that it was left dented.

Know this, breathe deep, put your armour back on and head out on your next adventure, keeping your head held high – there are over seven billion people on Planet Earth right now.

You got this.

# DISAGREEING WITH THE ONES WE LOVE

**Communication and patience are our best tools when it comes to disagreement with those we love.**

## COMMUNICATION TOOLS

- Put yourself in the other person's shoes and try to understand why they're saying what they are saying.

- Think of ways round expressing your particular opinion without getting angry. Shouting never works.

- Come up with different ways of explaining whatever it is that you are disagreeing about. A letter? A discussion at a later date?

- And, in the meantime, it might be good to get someone else's opinion.

## PATIENCE

- Refer to the point opposite on 'discussion at a later date'.

- Time, which comes up a lot in this book, is a magical thing.

- Over time, things can inexplicably fall into place.

- Time really does heal. Patience applied to a disagreement with someone can work wonders.

# TOXIC LOVE AND ABUSIVE RELATIONSHIPS

In a 2009 NSPCC survey, one-quarter of girls aged thirteen to seventeen reported experiencing intimate partner violence; one in nine female respondents had experienced severe physical violence; and almost three-quarters of girls had experienced emotional abuse.*

From the age of twelve to seventeen, I was with a boy, the same age as me, who I felt truly, madly, deeply for. We lived every day in the moment, kissed more than anyone's ever kissed, and would've glued ourselves to one another if we could. It was fast, it was ferocious and it was a furious kind of love. It was my first love, which I don't necessarily believe is the best as they say, but I do believe it is the most confusing.

I was young, filled with feelings and learning how to steer it all, how to motor along and function in life as smoothly as I could. Sometimes it was really, really good – and sometimes it was really, really bad. Sometimes we'd argue so much he'd get really angry; he'd smack my head against the wall in his bedroom. Or he'd squeeze my thigh so hard under the table to secretly threaten me that it would bruise.

What I couldn't identify at the time was that I was in a DAMAGING and ABUSIVE relationship. I felt so wrapped up in my own world and in our own moment that when these bad things happened, all I wanted most in the world was for him to say sorry (which he never did). I didn't think about how it would make me feel years later, after we'd broken up. I had no idea that what was going on with us was proper abuse – at the time, the only abuse I saw represented anywhere was related to older people, married couples, mostly on soaps like *Brookside*. I never saw anything I identified with – nothing that showed my situation.

I was fifteen. I had no idea of the seriousness. I wish someone could've told me how bad it was, that I was letting him do this to me over and over. I wish someone could've told me that it wasn't my fault and that I didn't deserve it. It took me finding him in bed with not one, but two other girls to finally break up with him. I'm ashamed to say – it wasn't even the violence. It was only years later that I realized how toxic he was for me.

I would NEVER let ANYONE use their physical strength against me ever, ever again.

I now passionately believe in high-lighting the issue of violent and abusive relationships amongst teenagers and young people.

*Abuse: to use (something) to bad effect or for a bad purpose; misuse.

A few years ago I was in a shop in East London – where I was living at the time – and I overheard a conversation between two schoolgirls about pop stars Rihanna and Chris Brown. It had recently been globally reported that Chris Brown (nineteen at the time) had attacked his then girlfriend Rihanna (twenty-one at the time) and left her face badly beaten.

'Did you hear about what happened to Rihanna?' said one of the girls.

'No. What happened?' asked her friend.

'Chris Brown beat the crap out of her,' the other responded nonchalantly.

'Bet she deserved it, the slag,' said her friend.

Hearing this conversation nearly made me burst into tears – it brought back how I had never taken my own abusive relationship seriously either. It made me want to investigate the attitudes of young people when it comes to what's OK, and what is not OK.

So I made a documentary about it for Radio 1. It was called 'Bruising Silence', and it focused on the nuances of abusive relationships, our understanding of them, and what defines abusive from a young person's perspective.

Making the documentary was as fascinating as it was sad. I interviewed many different people on the subject of abusive relationships. I learned that unfortunately there are many different foul flavours of abuse.

Abuse does not discriminate and can happen in all types of relationships, including same-sex relationships.

- A female can be the abuser as well as a male.
- It can be nearly impossible to detect subtle abuse, the type that is more mental rather than physical or verbal.
- Abuse has many layers and can make someone feel powerless.
- Abuse can even exist in loving relationships.

**All abuse is very serious. I want you to know that if someone is hurting you, mentally or physically, it is not right and that you must seek extra help.**

# WHAT DOES COERCIVE MEAN?

'Coercive' is a word describing a form of control of a dysfunctional nature. It is associated with threats, and bullying. Someone in a coercive relationship may not be able to recognize the signs easily and it can be done in a swirl of seemingly gentle ways. Like when someone makes you feel like you 'HAVE TO . . .' do something, go somewhere, be a certain way. If you are ever feeling you 'HAVE TO . . .' any of these things ask yourself who's applying the pressure and how often that happens.

It is not easy to understand the curves and the bends of relationships, but 'stock checks' are important. Assessing if you're genuinely happy most of the time needs to happen lots, even in the most loving of relationships.

## Women's Aid says:

If you think you might be in an abusive relationship, remember you are not on your own and it is not your fault. You can go to www.lovedontfeelbad.co.uk to find out more about different forms of abuse, including coercive and controlling behaviour, and how you can get support and information. You can also go to the main Women's Aid website – www.womensaid.org.uk – to visit our Survivors' Forum, where you can speak to others who have experienced abuse in a relationship, or call the National Domestic Violence Helpline on 0808 2000 247, which runs in partnership with Women's Aid and Refuge.

# HEARTBREAK

## ACHY BREAKY HEART

Most of the human race has experienced heartache. MILLIONS of people have had their hearts broken. It's a completely normal part of life, and an important part too. Artists, poets and musicians have done their best work during or after heartbreak (more on this later). Heartbreak means you are ALIVE. You feel things. And you will grow through it all. It makes you the amazing person you are, one who has empathy and compassion.

# THE RULES OF HEARTBREAK AND HEARTACHE

**A HEART can ACHE
for a number of reasons.**

Injustice in the world

A natural disaster

A smell

A movie

A song

A letter

Loss

**And A HEART can BREAK because of
a number of triggers.**

A person or an animal you love dying

A person betraying you

A friend dropping you

Global tragedies such as wars, terrorism,
droughts, poverty or accidents

Anyone you care for being seriously ill

Being dumped

**And HOW does it FEEL?**

Like your world has caved in

Like a part of you is missing

Like the sun has gone in forever

Like happiness will never come back

Like a pain in your chest, or your stomach

Like your tears will never stop

## It HURTS SO BAD.

**But it WILL get better. And it
will not kill you – it will make
you stronger.**

# HEARTBREAK CAN...

- **turn you into a bit of beast,** a crying, snotty, wailing heartbreak monster – a stomping, angry, wild thing.

- **make you react extremely emotionally** to songs that wouldn't usually affect you.

- **do the same as above, but with sad or romantic films,** especially on planes for some reason. You can find yourself on a flight with an uncontrollably tear-drenched face (this has happened to me SO many times).

- **dent your pride.** You'll find that your ego is at a loose end when breaking up, even though sometimes a relationship just simply ISN'T RIGHT.

- **make you lose your appetite.** But please do eat – it'll make you feel better. Eat some ice cream.

- **confuse the hell out of you.** It's even possible to fancy someone harder when they are unattainable – a cruel and twisted element of fate.

- **make you engage in some hard snogging with your ex,** even though you are likely to crash and burn afterwards.

- **chemically imbalance you.** Some research has shown that breaking up with someone can be similar to the feeling of withdrawing from actual drugs. GAHHHH.

- **hurt.** It's been proven that heartbreak can create a physical pain and discomfort, like a tight chest, stomach pain or headache.

- **make you go off the things you used to love,** like sunshine, or chips.

- **radically change your appearance,** or cause you to take up exercise obsessively, anything to distract yourself!

- **give you the most refreshing newfound sense of independence.**

- **make you wiser and stronger.**

# AND CAN'T DO

## HEARTBREAK CAN'T...

- **stay forever.**

- **stop you from fancying someone else.**

- **stop you from being clever and funny and creative,** or good at maths. You are bright like a spark – if not brighter now.

- **be shaken off easily.** Give yourself the time you need to heal. Time will make it easier, and sometimes a good actual shake is worth a try.

- **be fully described in emoji form.** If you are ready to use these to describe how you feel, I reckon you're feeling a bit better.

- **always be completely understood by everyone around you.** Sometimes our mates and family members just won't understand how we feel. Don't expect everyone to always get it.

- **stop you from being beautiful.** You are still beautiful.

- **stop the world from spinning on its axis.** Even though it feels like the world doesn't look the same during heartbreak, it is still there, waiting for you.

- **sink your boat.** It's been rocked, but it can't sink it.

| Pharmacy Stamp | Age | Title, Forename, Surname & Address |
| --- | --- | --- |
| | D.O.B. | |

Number of days' treatment
N.B. Ensure dose is stated

Endorsements

**SYMPTOMS:** Loud crying, hyper sensitivity, feeling sorry for yourself and wrapping yourself up into a hedgehog-like ball.

**DIRECTIONS:** Invite every single one of your friends to your house immediately, moan about your heartbreak till you have no words left. Then cover your face in glitter and go out disco-dancing in the sparkliest outfit you own, and dance till it feels like your legs might drop off.

**REPEAT EVERY WEEKEND TILL YOU ARE FEELING BETTER.**

| Signature of Prescriber | Date |
| --- | --- |

For dispenser No. of Prescns. on form

*Gemma Cairney*

# YOUR HEARTACHE PLAYLIST

**Melt into the magic of music with a specially prepared HEARTBREAK PLAYLIST.**

## For a good cry

1. 'Thinkin' 'Bout You' – Frank Ocean
2. 'Never Ever' – All Saints
3. 'Don't Speak' – No Doubt
4. 'Radio Silence' – James Blake
5. 'No Room for Doubt' by Lianne La Havas and Willy Mason
6. 'Mood Indigo' – Nina Simone

## For hopes and boogies

1. 'Daydreamer' – Adele
2. 'Tears Dry On Their Own' – Amy Winehouse
3. 'Shake It Out' – Florence and The Machine
4. 'Shackles' – Mary Mary
5. 'Heartbreaker' – Mariah Carey
6. 'Shine On' – Roses
7. 'Dancing On My Own' – Robyn

# Help for heartache

Most heartache will pass, but if you are finding it VERY difficult to move forward and feel stuck with your feelings, or if you are worried about your mental health, head to the 'YOUR MIND' section of this book. **Always ask for help.**

# DEATH, LOSS AND GRIEF

# A RICH AND CONFUSING PAIN

We can learn a lot about how we feel about life from death. Death can make you angrier and more confused and helpless than anything else. Death leaves us desperate. It is the one inevitable truth about life. It is the darkest of dark, the biggest blow – the deepest.

The fear of death is in most of us. It's hard to admit – if we admit it, it may envelop our entire being and we won't be able to shake the thought. Fear of being alone, fear of loss, fear of fear.

# WHEN SOMEBODY DIES

Grief is as individual as we are. There is no right way to do it. No right or wrong feeling. When somebody you love dies, the first thing you feel is shock, even if you know it is coming. You might feel nothing at first, and that is OK. Let yourself work through it at your own pace. If you want to cry, feel free to stoop your head, and give yourself to the sadness.

I will never forget the puddles of tears and sticky wet faces during the periods of bereavement in my life. It hurts like a dagger to lose someone. It hurts to watch others hurting who've lost someone too. I've always found a warmth in togetherness during these times. To know that neither I nor whoever it is that's lost someone close to them is alone.

I don't think the hurt ever completely goes away. But time makes it less raw. I promise you. Never, ever forget that there is someone out there that wants to soothe your ache. There are people who will open their ears to you no matter how bleak you feel.

No right or wrong feeling

# TRYING TOO HARD TO GET OVER IT

Feeling like you have to be fine straight away, bounce back and get on with work and normal life can affect you later down the line. Ride the waves of your heart, check in with yourself daily. You might feel completely different day by day or hour by hour, and people around you will just have to go with it. If you feel like you need some time to yourself, you need it.

On the other hand, wanting to be happy again is not wrong either. It is also completely normal. You have a life to live, and if something makes you giggle that is all right, that's what the person you've lost would've wanted – for you to still know what it's like to giggle. Don't ever feel guilty about how you feel – guilt is a waste of time.

# WHAT TO EXPECT

I talked to a young woman called Frances Acquaah, who is the primary carer for her younger brother and sister since the death of her dad six years ago, and her mother more recently. Frances opened up to me about her experiences.

'Time is a healer,' says Frances. 'Many people will tell you. I found this especially annoying because I couldn't see past how I felt in that very moment. Take it each day at a time. Do not let anyone rush you or tell you how you should feel. Whilst I don't believe there is a "one size fits all" guide of what to expect, here are a few things I experienced after losing my parents.'

# CHANGE

'When you lose someone, especially someone that you love or are close to, everything changes. In my personal experience, there is no way you can be prepared for this, even if this person's death was expected.

'When my mother passed away, everything changed. Most of it was stuff that was out of my control, and it was challenging to adjust to my new life and responsibilities. It's so easy to bury your head under the sand – as I did initially – but the longer you do this, the harder it will be when you have to face your new realities.

'Whilst it's important to take time out and address your feelings, it's equally important to have someone around to keep your affairs in order until you're ready.'

# ANXIETY

'I avoided social situations for a long time. I didn't want people to tell me they were "sorry" and I hated the way people treated me with pity. Apart from this, my emotions were unpredictable. I could feel completely numb one day, and spend the next week crying myself to sleep. I'm the type of person that likes to block things out (I wouldn't advise anyone to do this, by the way), but I've been learning to accept how I feel in every moment, even if that means crying in public! Remember you are a human being and not a robot.'

## DENIAL

'Dealing with grief when you are young, it can be hard to accept that they are gone. Denial is often spoken about as a key stage of the grieving process, and it is definitely something I've encountered more so the second time around.

'I was seventeen when my father died. He wasn't very well, so it was a lot easier to accept his death over my mother's, whom I was closer to. Sometimes I just sit in disbelief, as I still can't believe she isn't here. I once even thought about ringing her to tell her something – then I remembered I couldn't.

'Even now, just over a year later, I tend to speak about my mum in the present tense. Is this healthy? I'm no expert, but this is how I feel comfortable talking about her for now, so that's what I'm going to do.'

## DEPRESSION

'I'm not sure what words can be used to accurately describe the feeling of losing someone you love. It's a heart-wrenching feeling that makes the world stop for you.

'I think it's important to seek help when you're feeling low, regardless of how you got to that place. But you have to be ready and open to receive help. Admitting it is the hardest part. Once you've done this, you are well on your way!

'Getting the help you need can often be a bit tricky, but don't be disheartened if your doctor fails you or if you are turned away – keep trying! Whilst counselling didn't solve my problems, I did, however, find it helpful to talk about how I was feeling and say the words out loud.'

# BEING THERE FOR YOUR GRIEVING FRIENDS

**It's not easy to know how to support people you love when they are grieving. Here's some useful advice of what to do, and what not to do.**

## Be positive

Don't project your fear of death on to them. Nobody who's recently lost someone wants to hear how much you'd hate it if it happened to you. Nor do they necessarily expect you to know exactly how it feels. The truth is you don't know exactly, because we're all different.

## Hug and comfort

Hug them tight and ask them if they are all right. Refer to the reading list for loss and grieving on page 56, and perhaps choose one book to give them as a gift?

## Listen

There is no right or wrong in the subject of dying – just keep close and listen to how they feel, and be prepared to feel stilted at points. No one has the answers, but those who are grieving don't want to feel ostracized for doing so.

56

# INGREDIENTS FOR A HAPPY HEART

**All you need for a happy heart is to approach life's situations with an OPEN heart. A heart full of empathy, kindness, compassion and hope.**

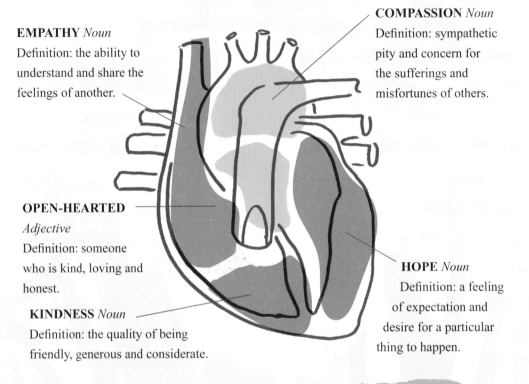

**EMPATHY** *Noun*
Definition: the ability to understand and share the feelings of another.

**COMPASSION** *Noun*
Definition: sympathetic pity and concern for the sufferings and misfortunes of others.

**OPEN-HEARTED**
*Adjective*
Definition: someone who is kind, loving and honest.

**KINDNESS** *Noun*
Definition: the quality of being friendly, generous and considerate.

**HOPE** *Noun*
Definition: a feeling of expectation and desire for a particular thing to happen.

# READING LIST FOR LOSS AND GRIEVING

*My Sister Lives on the Mantlepiece* by Annabel Pitcher
*Unboxed* by Non Pratt
*The Square Root of Summer* by Harriet Reuter Hapgood
*I'll Give You the Sun* by Jandy Nelson
*The Sky Is Everywhere* by Jandy Nelson
*The Five Stages of Andrew Brawley* by Shaun David Hutchinson
*The Year of the Rat* by Clare Furniss
*A Monster Calls* by Patrick Ness

For any more information on bereavement and grief, turn to the back of this book, and you will find organizations there to help you through it.

# YOUR BODY
# † SOUL

# INTRODUCTION

Our BODIES – the ships that carry our cargo of thoughts, feelings, loves and anxieties through the world. Alive and kicking. Even though they are amazing machines, we often find it all too easy to be at war with our bodies, or feel trapped inside them. In this part of the book, we will explore how this can happen, and assess how it might be possible to love our bodies more. Because they are all – without exception – REMARKABLE.

Your body is an extraordinary, living, breathing, fantastical mass of cells, which people spend years and years studying to understand. Your body can do so many amazing things. It can even heal itself. Isn't that mind-blowing?

Our SOULS. Imagine an immensely deep, glistening wishing well – the type of well you can imagine spouting a rainbow. Our souls are OUR wells: the core of who we really are. Our soul is our personality, our feeling-holder, our gut instinct, our individual spirit, the part of us that makes us feel happy and alive. The best thing about souls is that there are no two the same. Your soul is wholly unique to you. It burns bright, with all the colours of the warmest flames. Our body and soul are so interconnected they blur and work together as one. In order to nurture our souls, we need to learn to love and understand our bodies.

With all this in mind, how do you feel in your soul about the way your body actually looks? Go and stand naked in front of a mirror. Are you aware of how wonderful its individualities are? Do you know its every crease? How have you felt about your body over the years? Has it changed? Do you remember finding your first pubes? (I recall the day I spent staring in disbelief at mine . . . I just couldn't believe that my body had grown such thick, curly black hair . . . down there.)

Then there is that defiant hair sprouting from your nipple . . . which keeps coming back, no matter how many times you pluck it out. (Yes – that can happen anywhere between your teens and your twenties and is completely NORMAL, so don't let anyone make you feel it isn't.) Pubes, creases, breasts and hips – they all appear just when you're feeling at your most self-conscious, and it can feel weird and uncomfortable. It's very easy to start scrutinizing and criticizing bits of yourself that are in fact bloody marvellous.

# I'm in Knee deep

For a flicker of time, I remember being absolutely infuriated by my knees. OK, so let me try to explain. Being mixed race means there are some parts of your body that are darker, more 'black', than others. In the gene pool, these things could have swung either way, but my knees are darker than the rest of my legs, and I also scar more easily. That is the way darker-pigmented skin is. A boyfriend once tactlessly asked me why I had what looked like 'muddy knees' in comparison to the rest of my body. I remember this getting me down, and I really disliked my knees for a bit. On reflection, I find this fact so ridiculous that I am almost ashamed to put it in this book. MY KNEES. I HAD A PROBLEM WITH MY KNEES. That boy didn't mean to be unkind, but it was kinda HIS problem, not MINE. Of course, my hang-ups didn't start and end there – but this is up there with the most ludicrous tripe I have ever thought about myself . . . and, trust me, there has been a LOT of ludicrous tripe along the way.

During my teens, I desperately wanted bigger boobs, and relentlessly eyeballed the money-making bullcrap of supposedly 'herbal' pills that promised to 'miraculously' and 'completely naturally' increase their size. What a load of money-making codswallop. I used to stand so close to the mirror that I convinced myself the hair on my top lip was actually going to get in the way of my life, that I was a freak of nature – never taking into consideration the fact that I was practically KISSING the mirror. If anyone was to ever get that close to my face, they'd probably have their eyes closed . . . COS THAT'S WHAT YOU DO TO SMOOCH for gyaaaad's sake.

I also had spots bad enough to be called acne. My entire forehead was decorated with pus-filled volcanoes; I wore ashy, fudge-brown foundation in an attempt to cover them up, which was often two or three shades too light – as back then (and still now) many high street, affordable make-up brands didn't have the right shades for my skin tone (they weren't stock priority for a town called Horsham in West Sussex, where I was one of only two black people at my school).

As an adult, I have harboured a deep desire for a tummy that doesn't protrude so much that people occasionally mistake its pokey-outness for pregnancy. (My tummy actually protrudes because I have a fibroid – a benign lump of useless muscle in my tummy – which would require the hassle of serious surgery to remove, and that I've been advised not to do if it doesn't cause me any trouble – which it doesn't right now.)

The times my confidence has been most challenged have all been to do with my career. When I landed my first job as a presenter in the outer space that my industry can sometimes represent, I found myself surrounded by people trying really hard to be a 'celebrity'. Despite the idea of being famous rendering me a flinching, gagging mess – there are certain dizzyingly glamorous elements of my job that are too fun to ignore. Like going to the Brit Awards, or sitting in the front row at a fashion show, or going to a party too swanker-dank-danky to turn down. There are those events where I am hardened by champagne promises and the plumes of a silent visual hierarchy cos the place is filled with pedigree-cat-like people who are so shiny that your jaw drops when you are near them. Women whose bodies are so waif-like you want to swaddle them in a blanket and feed them like you would if you found a small bird.

So, yeah, I've wondered before whether it'd be worth changing my lifestyle: losing the freedom I enjoy from indulging in all types of food, exercising as a priority over a lie-in, or getting on with some work – like starting my own production company or writing or pitching radio documentaries – or instead of meeting a friend I love for a drink and chat. But that JUST AIN'T ME. A me that tried to fit into a 'celebrity' mould would mean a very unhappy me.

After nearly a decade of working in a job that means I am occasionally in the public eye, I have received abuse on Twitter for 'not being able to talk properly', and for the colour of my skin, and, worse still, been told by a production company that I'm not 'girly' enough to even screen-test for a job I'm experienced enough to do.

All things considered, I feel unbelievably lucky to have grown up without the everyday annoyances and insecurities I have about my body (or the things other people have said to me about my body) ever causing me to drift into unhealthy territory. I don't know if it is because I was a teen before Instagram and selfie culture, but I was blissfully unaware of the size of my body in comparison to others. I never felt fat or thin; I didn't talk about weight with my friends. Without the constant sharing of photographs in the public arena, without the invitation to judge our bodies given to every stranger on the internet, my friends and I were able to happily exist without comparing ourselves to other women.

Don't get me wrong, 'body dysmorphia' – a term used for a corrupted sense of the shape or size of your body – has always existed, but now more than ever it seems that this negative relationship with our bodies has become almost acceptable . . . normal, even.

I thoroughly err on the 'f*ck it' side of life. I love my body, its caramel colour, and its willingness to dance and wiggle to all music. I love my boobs (which grew in the end, to two perfectly round jam-doughnut-sized jigglers). I love that these legs have walked me up the 5,188 metres of Mount Kenya, cycled me from London to Paris, jumped me into the sea where I live. I love my face and its mixed-racedness, the unpredictability of my tightly coiled afro hair. My body is me. My body is a punk that will be clothed in whatever I'm in the mood for. I have not been on the front of magazines, like some of the TEENY TINY crew. I do not fit into the cookie cutter of the who's who of the famous and cool. But I am happy. And that makes me lucky.

What WORRIES me is that now I feel like I'm constantly hearing from people dealing with deep-rooted feelings of hate for their bodies, leading to obsessive dieting, cosmetic surgery or self-harm. If you are feeling a sadness towards your body, you are definitely not alone. I hope that reading about it will help you feel like you can talk about and explore all these feelings and start loving your body.

The feeling of not looking right is backed up by magazine covers, Insta-followers, the sense that SKINNY = better. I can see why and how this affects our sense that our own bodies aren't right. Celebrity is a simmering pot of false truths when it comes to representing life. If you entertain the celebrity lifestyle as aspirational, it is near impossible not to be sucked into thinking you have to be a certain type of skinny and play the game by representing yourself in a certain way to be accepted.

Please, BE KIND to yourself and to others: it will pour into your smile. It'll make you dazzle, glisten and shine. A smile is what should be promoted on EVERYTHING. A true smile is sexier, cooler, more aspirational than any thigh gap on the planet.

64

# YOUR REMARKABLE BODY

The first step towards loving your body is understanding how special it is. Our bodies are as remarkable as we are fragile, and it's time to celebrate, explore and enjoy our bodies while we can.

I talked to the incredible Professor Hugh Montgomery, a man who knows a lot about bodies.

He's not only the director of the Institute for Human Health and Performance at University College London, but he also holds the world record for underwater piano playing!

I asked him some questions in a mission to discover just how magnificent human bodies are.

## Tell us something we don't know about a part of the body.

The heart isn't just a pump. It is FOUR pumps joined together, with its own electrical wiring system. It pumps enough blood to fill an Olympic swimming pool every year.

## Is it true that many people reading this will live to over one hundred?

Yes. Life expectancy has been rising steadily in the last half-century or more, and many now live to one hundred. When I was a junior doctor back in 1990, anyone over the age of sixty-five went to the 'geriatric' team. None of us would class someone of sixty-five as 'old' any more!

## If we were to have a party to celebrate the human body, and I asked everyone to come dressed as their favourite body part, which would you come as and why?

That's hard. I guess coming dressed as a muscle would be hard. But the joy of being able to exercise – run, jump, dance – depends on good muscles, bones and joints. Likewise, the brain brings the joy of consideration, problem-solving and more. But every organ is truly remarkable – and one doesn't have to look very hard to see that.

WOW. You're feeling quite impressed with your body now, aren't you? Good, because it is a simply incredible, messy, pulsating, super-smart machine.

# PERIODS

At some point during puberty, a girl's body starts preparing itself for egg fertilization, and this happens EVERY SINGLE MONTH, for decades. The uterus is quite the relentless queen in her mission to get a fertilized egg. Its lining gets thicker every monthly cycle, essentially in preparation for pregnancy. If no fertilized egg ends up there, which (among other reasons) happens when the egg does not meet a viable sperm, the uterus lining is shed through the vagina. This process is officially known as MENSTRUATION, more commonly known as having a PERIOD.

# THE BLOODY NUMBERS

On average, each of those born female will have around 480 periods in their life.

A ballpark of 334 million of the world's population are having their periods right now.

Periods last anything from 2 to 7 days.

The average menstruator spends thousands on disposable products, and throws away 11,000 pads or tampons into landfills throughout their reproductive lifetime.

One egg is released from a woman's body 12 to 14 days after an actual period, during the time that is known as ovulation.

On average, 2.4 tablespoons of actual blood is lost during the menstrual cycle, and a further 1 to 6 tablespoons of menstrual fluid.

(Don't know about you, but it often feels like enough to fill six 2-litre cola bottles to me!)

Until the year 2000, tampons incurred a 17.5 per cent tax in the UK.

If you are a trans guy or a proud uterus owner who identifies as non-binary, genderfluid or agender, check out page 84, which talks about including menstruators of all genders.

In Burkina Faso, 83 per cent of girls have nowhere to change their sanitary menstrual materials (source: Unicef).

The average menstrual cycle may be longer or shorter than 28 days - anywhere from 21 to 35 is pretty normal!

(Anyone else worry they were pregnant on day 29 just because you hadn't got your period yet? Just me?!!!) If you want to know what the average is for you, chart your cycle! Use your phone calendar, diary, or one of a zillion apps out there. Clue is a great app because it's not sponsored by a tampon company trying to grab your cash. It gives you a place to record loads of cool stats, it's nicely designed and it's not so pink and stereotypically girly that you'll want to vom!

AND SO. IT'S HAPPENING. Periods are a THING, but NO ONE EVER TALKS ABOUT THEM. Rather than create embarrassment, let's turn it into wonderment – periods are part of the whole business of creating human life, after all. V. COOL.

We all experience menstruation differently – for some, periods are light and pain-free; for others, they are heavier and cause cramping and bloating. Occasionally periods can be made very painful and last longer than normal because of underlying conditions such as endometriosis. If you are suffering badly and for longer than is normal, please talk to your parent or guardian and your doctor. It is very unlikely there is something seriously wrong, but by talking about it you will get the help you need to get through your period.

Periods are the great female equalizer, and practically everyone has an embarrassing period tale. I think that by sharing our stories we can lose the dread that comes with the prospect of a leak. It's crap if it happens to you, but remember that you're not alone! Here's my story . . .

## THE WORST LEAK OF MY LIFE

I started my periods when I was twelve, and I'll never forget having to use the staff loos at school to change my sanitary towel for the first time. On that note, why are they called that? 'Sanitary towel' sounds so clinical. SO embarrassing. That's exactly how periods are marketed, isn't it? All the packaging – way too PINK, vagina-shaming and EMBARRASSING . . . Anyway, over the subsequent years, I thought I had got a grip on the monthly blood-fest. On the advice of my mum, I had 'graduated' to tampons. I was a period 'pro', head held high in the air. Granted, the pains were like a war in my womb and made me vomit – but I was holding it down, this period malarkey.

Fast-forward to me aged seventeen at a birthday party. I was twisting and shouting the night away, at a party – beneath rainbow disco lights, lost in a cloud of R'n'B and twirly good times – with the boyfriend who made my heart pound harder than anyone had before. I was on fire. I had on my dream dress: it was from Tammy (a shop that was the bee's knees for teens everywhere in the nineties and early noughties – a bit like Topshop is today). It was a reversible satin dress with bra-like straps instead of normal ones – all adjustable and suggestive. This dress was SO good, stretchy satin, clingy, classy – AND, as it was reversible, either burgundy or black; I'd gone for chic black. A safe option, as I was on my period and I wouldn't have to fear leaking.

Anyway, there I was in my Tammy dress feeling damned fine and period-pain free. Everything felt so good, so unlimited. We danced till closing, around midnight. We were not in the mood for this night to end. How could it? It was fun of the best type. There I was perched on my boyfriend's lap, holding court amongst a rabble of lads, booming with laughter and sweat . . . till the lights came on, and the cheesiest of cheese DJs announced on the mic that it was time to leave. The party was over, and it was time for everyone to stop chasing dreams and go home. We didn't want to, but we pushed out giggles to the ultimate maximum, and then . . .

Then I stood up, removed myself from my boyfriend's lap, glanced down and saw the equivalent of all my nightmares coming true. There on my beloved's lap, on his off-white chinos, was a distinct puddle of BLOOD. I had leaked period blood, but had been too sweaty and happy to notice before. Worse still, the lights were up bright – as bright could be – and EVERYONE could see, staring in disbelief at the red stain on my boy's trousers. My eyes were hot with tears. I was a husk, my self-confidence blown away in a matter of seconds. My eyes met my boyfriend's, desperate for security and a sign of hope. I couldn't speak: embarrassment had rendered me speechless.

'Hahahahahahahhahahahahaha,' squealed my friend Miriam. 'If you'd rubbed the other way, you'd have made the perfect England flag.'

It goes without saying that my boyfriend was not pleased. Beat that for the worst leak of your life.

See, MANY of us have been victims of the unexpected gush of the messy period. Many of us have been caught unawares by a sudden blood waterfall at the most inconvenient time and wearing the most inappropriate clothes. Periods are often cheeky and unpredictable. But if it happens to you, it's not the end of the world. One day you'll look back on it and laugh!

# Tips + tales from da gals

'Please make sure you tell everyone not to wear a sanitary towel and go swimming,' said one of my mates when I asked her about a period she'd rather forget. 'I put two sanitary towels in my swimming costume to protect me from any leakage . . . only to find that, once I'd gone down the first water slide, they'd BOTH inflated in between my legs to the size of a small arm-band in my crotch. I literally had to put my hands in front of the bulge and run to the toilet to sort it out.'

'The worst is when you go to another country and you have come on, and you're, like, Where are the tampons? Where am I? What's going on? AND it's, like, twenty minutes before I'm going on live TV. And you're, like, Arrrrrghhhhh. I'm leaking through my fishnets!' – Marawa the Amazing, world-famous hula-hooper.

Feel free to write or draw your depiction of THE WORST LEAK YOU'VE EVER HAD. It might feel good to get it down. Go into as much or as little detail as you want.

# IF YOU'RE A BOY AND WANT TO KNOW MORE ABOUT PERIODS, HERE ARE SOME DOS AND DON'TS

 find out about the menstrual cycle and how it works.

 ask your school to include boys in lessons on periods – and if there are no lessons, demand them!

 find out about the different types of menstruation management (tampons, etc.) so you can get used to them if a friend or family member wants you to buy or borrow some for them.

 squirm at any sign of period paraphernalia. If a girl leaves a tampon wrapper on the side in the bathroom, or whatever – give her a break. There's quite a lot of fiddling around that's involved in a period.

 tease someone if they leak blood through their clothes (or on your clothes!) – play it cool and help them out.

 assume someone is 'on their period' if they are in a bad mood with you. It's more likely you've wound them up all by yourself, and mentioning periods will NOT do you any favours.

 assume that if someone's on their period they can't get pregnant – you can get pregnant if you're ovulating, and some people ovulate more than once in a month every now and then!

If you are feeling a bit like you can't talk about your period to anybody and you are often grossed out by it, it's time to work out how to navigate your way through this biologically brilliant but messy time of the month. How chilled are you about the blob? (Yes, that is possibly the world's WORST way to describe it. That and 'on the red'. Though my favourite has got to be 'surfing the crimson wave', thanks to the legendary film *Clueless*, which, if you haven't watched it – YOU MUST!)

# PMT

Just before your period, you can feel pretty different to your usual self . What a horrible debbie-downing-mother-trucker PMT (pre-menstrual tension, also known as PMS, where the 'S' stands for 'syndrome') can be. How dare it! How dare it mess with us so vigorously that it feels like someone's turned us quite literally upside down?

Mood swings? For some, it's more like a 'mood tsunami'. One of the most annoying things about PMT is how easy it is to forget about it once a period is all over. Once the crimson tide has been surfed, your body forgets the pain and the emotional rawness as quickly as it was knocked for six in the first place. For most of us, we just have to get used to it, know it's going to come and accept that it probably won't last very long. If, however, your PMT is lasting longer than two weeks and starting to really get you down, talk to your doctor about it. It's a natural companion to periods – before and during – but it is always good to get some expert advice if you're worried.

# THE PAIN

PERIOD PAIN SUCKS. Like little weights dangling from your ovaries, creating a dull and sometimes agonizing ache. My periods have become better over the years – more level and controllable, as long as I time the painkillers for when the clock strikes 'PERIOD'. But when I was younger I used to get pain so bad I had to leave lessons, as nothing could stop me being physically sick. If you get terrible period pain, I feel for you. It's a cliché, but a hot-water bottle really helps, and speak to your doctor if your period pain is starting to get in the way of your life. Periods are complex, but there are many ways to make them better, and your GP might have some of those answers – just be vocal.

75

# PERIOD QUIZ, ANYONE?

**When buying menstrual products, do you:**

**A** Either use reusables and tell your friends all about them, or boldly festoon the checkout till with your monthly supply of sanitary products, proud as punch, and don't ask for a bag to hide them in?

**B** Feel flushed and agitated, but know that it's essential and a fact of life?

**C** Get your mum, sister or even your dad to do it because you cannot bear to buy them yourself?

**You get bad cramps every month – how do you deal with it?**

**A** It's awful, but you've spoken to lots of people around you about how it affects you specifically, so everybody can try to understand when it's at its worst.

**B** You stock up on pain relief, put a brave face on it and only complain to your closest mates.

**C** You don't tell a soul, even if it really hurts, because you would rather die than let anyone know you are on your period. You hope nothing worse is wrong, but are afraid to mention it to your doctor.

**When heading to the loo during your time of the month, you:**

**A** Are happy to openly grab a tampon or pad out of your bag, and see no shame in anyone seeing it in your hand as you stroll on over.

**B** Furtively stuff your tampon or pad up your sleeve.

**C** Have a special discreet pouch in your bag for disguising your menstrual products so it looks like you're going to put make-up on.

**What is a Mooncup?**

**A** A brand name for a menstrual cup – a reusable alternative to tampons or sanitary towels/pads, which is made of a small silicone cup that is inserted into your vagina.

**B** A barometer that looks a bit like a dreamcatcher, used by hippies to judge when a period is due according to the alignment of the stars.

**C** A red mug with a moon picture on it.

**You're worried you've leaked all over your light jeans at a barbecue. What do you do?**

**A** Ask the mates you are sitting with to check as you stand up and to holler 'CODE RED' if it's happened.

**B** Wrap your jacket round your waist, stand up really quickly and scuttle to the loo to check.

**C** Disregard this question, as you only wear black during your period.

**In a bid to raise awareness for women around the world who have no access to feminine hygiene products, Kiran Gandhi made the headlines when she ran the London Marathon in 2015. What did she do?**

**A** Free bleeding (meaning she was on her period and ran without protection).

**B** Dressed up as a tampon.

**C** You don't even wanna know if it's got ANYTHING to do with periods.

*77*

**When asked why she appeared ill after a race at the Olympics in Rio 2016, Fu Yuanhui, the bronze-medal-winning Olympic swimmer from China, said in an interview that her stomach pain was due to:**

**A** Menstrual cramps, which made her tired after her race, although she said it was not an excuse.

**B** Swimming in a white suit and swim cap with a string attached, to protest the lack of tampon use in China.

**C** You don't want to know, and hope it has nothing to do with periods because, eww.

## Mostly As: The Magnificent Menstruator

GURL, you are owning menstruation. You are fearless, have embraced your monthly cycle and realize that communication and expressiveness when it comes to periods is a healthy thing. You may be interested in the 'Period Activism' movements emerging online.

## Mostly Bs: The Period Tolerater

You are the most common type of menstruator. You are aware and accept the fact that you have a period once a month – though you still find it an embarrassing fact of the female condition. You may want to check out Chella Quint's TEDx Talk 'Adventures in Menstruating' – it's very eye opening about menstrual taboos from history! (bit.ly/periodpositive)

## Mostly Cs: The Period Denier

You're mortified by your periods and wish they never happened. But it's not your fault – and there's stuff you can do! Maybe the way you learned about them was tough going, or too little, too late. Or maybe you had to figure it out for yourself. Adverts don't help, that's for sure. You've never found the right language to discuss them, and often feel stifled and ashamed when thinking about them. It could be worthwhile exploring why you feel like this and try to find someone you can confide in when it comes to your monthly cycle. Talking about menstruation turns the subject from taboo to normal. Remember: there are currently around 334 million people on their periods as you are reading this. We need to find a way to talk through our period worries and personal experiences with one another. Check out www.periodpositive.com for a crash course in shame-free menstruation.

# WHAT IS PERIOD ACTIVISM?

Period activism is a proactive movement to expose and combat the fact that periods are still very much stigmatized all over the world. There are now many 'movements' discussing menstruation frankly and openly online and beyond – from performance artists making statements in bloodied pants, to those shining a light on the lack of menstrual hygiene management in some poorer parts of the world.

Good hashtags to search on Twitter and Instagram for this are #PeriodChat and #PeriodPositive.

#PERIOD POSITIVE

#PERIOD CHAT

79

This section has been put together by the brilliant Chella Quint, comedian, menstruation education researcher and founder of #periodpositive. She presented an awesome TEDx Talk: Adventures in Menstruating: Don't Use Shame to Sell. (link again – bit.ly/periodpositive)

So there are four types of menstrual products. For real! You were probably thinking there were just two – pads and tampons, right? Most people – even parents and teachers, and definitely advertisers – tend to mention just these two! But there are four! Here's how I like to break it down . . .

**Menstrual products can be:**

**Internal** – worn inside your vagina.
**External** – worn inside your underwear, but outside your vagina.
**Disposable** – bought, worn once and then thrown away.
**Reusable** – bought, worn once, washed, dried and used again and again – for years!

Now – if you're seeing that reusable one and freaking out, you're not alone – but don't panic. We wash and reuse things that get stuff from our bodies on them all the time. We wash kitchen cutlery, mugs and glasses – and those get our spit on them. We wash our underwear and bed sheets too! . . . Unless you only wear disposable underwear, and your bed sheets come in a giant paper-towel roll, which you bin every morning, that is?!

So now that's cleared up, here are the four types again, along with the pros and cons of each one.

**Internal** (tampons, menstrual cups): You wear them inside your body so you can go swimming and – if you are a fashion maven – wear tight clothes without VMPL (visible menstrual product line!). On the negative side, some people don't like inserting tampons or menstrual cups into their vaginas – either they find it uncomfortable

generally, or they just haven't got the hang of it yet.

**External** (disposable pads and cloth pads): These are great for when you first start menstruating,

# TAMPONS

and some people swear by them for their whole lives. They can be more comfortable to wear when sleeping, and are easier to change without getting blood on your fingers. Some people find that pads feel really uncomfortable, a bit like a full nappy, when they get full of blood, though. And like our friend above, who learned the hard way . . . you definitely can't wear them swimming.

**Disposable** (disposable pads and tampons): They are convenient to get from a friend or quickly nip to the shop and buy if your period shows up a day early and you don't have a menstrual cup or cloth pad on you. They are expensive – some big-brand companies make huge profits, and use those profits to make loads of adverts . . . to sell more pads and tampons. It's a massive industry.

**Reusable** (cloth pads and menstrual cups): Good for the environment and for your wallet! One pad costs about the same as a box of disposable pads, but you can wash it, dry it and keep it for years. Menstrual cups come in different sizes to suit different body types and vagina shapes – and most companies have good return policies if they don't work for you. Cloth pads come in the same shapes, lengths and styles as disposable pads, but in way cuter patterns! You can't throw them away – so if you change it when you're out, you need to carry the used one in your handbag (in a ziplock bag or a small Tupperware box, or similar) until you get home and can put it in the wash.

Since all four types have different pros and cons, you might prefer to use a combination – maybe cloth pads at home at night; your menstrual cup during the day and on holiday; tampons in a pinch, when you realize you don't have your usual supplies with you; and disposable pads or pantyliners if your period means you're sensitive down there, or just don't feel like using something internally that day!

# SANITARY TOWELS

# TOXIC SHOCK SYNDROME

## What is it?

Toxic Shock Syndrome is a very rare but potentially life-threatening condition. It is caused by specific bacteria invading and releasing toxins into the bloodstream. TSS cases can occur in women, men and children. TSS can tend occur from localised infections like skin infections or in women who are having their periods and using tampons. TSS, although rare, is a medical emergency and it is important to have the knowledge about the symptoms and signs so you can seek early diagnosis and treatment.

Once TSS is diagnosed, emergency treatment of the bacterial infection with antibiotics and supportive treatment will be given in hospital to help your body cope with the toxins.

If you do use tampons, then it is really important to be aware of TSS and to be vigilant if you develop any symptoms of TSS and seek help immediately.

In general, if you are using tampons and suddenly get a high fever, aches, a rash, or flu-like symptoms, see your doctor immediately, because, while it's rare, TSS can go from looking like a simple illness to a really serious medical emergency very quickly, and you are way better safe than sorry!

**Here are the symptoms:**

**Sudden high temperature**
**Flu-like symptoms** – headache, cough, sore throat, muscle aches
**Vomiting and/or nausea**
**Dizziness, fainting or feeling faint**
**Diarrhoea**
**A rash** – a bit like sunburn
**Confusion**

If you develop any of these symptoms, you should contact a medical professional straight away to get their advice.

# Advice from Dr Radha - my co-host on the Radio 1 *Surgery*, and all-round, energy-bringing beam of love - on what you should do if you think you've left a tampon in for too long

Change your tampon every four to six hours and never leave a tampon in for more than eight hours.

The best thing to do is to remove it as soon as you can if you think it has been in for too long.

You can normally feel the string or tampon to remove it yourself on most occasions. Sometimes it helps to put one leg up on a toilet seat and breathe in and out to relax when you are trying to find it.

Sometimes you cannot find the string or it is difficult to feel the tampon as it can move further up your vagina. If this is the case, then contact your GP straight away or the NHS helpline 111. They will endeavour to remove it immediately. If it is out of hours, then call the Out Of Hours GP helpline in your area or call 111, or attend A&E for help to remove the tampon straight away.

**Tampon Tips**

- Consider setting an alarm on your phone to remind you to remove your tampon.

- Never use more than one tampon at a time.

- Always wash your hands before changing your tampon and after.

- Always try to use the lowest absorbency for your period flow.

- Get to know your tampon brand and read the leaflet inside the pack.

- It is useful to think about alternating between tampons and pads while you have your period.

- Before you go to sleep while being on your period always think about putting in a fresh tampon and removing it as soon as you wake up.

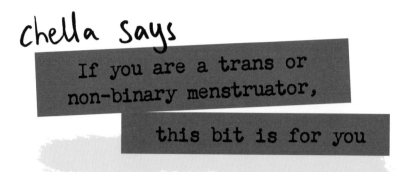

## chella Says

### If you are a trans or non-binary menstruator, this bit is for you

Not everyone who menstruates is a girl. And not all girls menstruate. If you're a trans guy or non-binary and you own a uterus, you have probably menstruated, or still do. You may not feel you fit into most conversations around menstruation, but there are loads of other trans and non-binary menstruators out there, and the conversation is (we agree, very slowly) changing. If you are out at school or college, and want to ensure you get support, ask friends, teachers and work colleagues of all genders to help you with the following:

* Use the word 'menstruator' to include everyone who menstruates.

* Try the phrases 'growing up' or 'going through puberty' or 'getting your first period' rather than saying someone is 'becoming a woman' to mean 'menstruating for the first time'.

* You might also consider asking that they re-label some toilets as unisex in your school, gig venue or workplace. If that's not possible right now, they should ensure there's a bin in cubicles in the gents' toilets as well, and that emergency menstrual products are available in there too.

# BODY HAIR

OH, body hair. The epidemic of angst towards our own body hair drives me absolutely bananas. I have personally spent years of calamitously razor-rashing my poor downstairs, or going to waxing salons so they can painfully strip it off. SO horrendously embarrassing, I actually shudder at the thought of some of those trips over the years. I take my hat off to anyone who's completely comfortable with getting out their most private and intimate body parts for someone to tweeze, pour hot wax over, and yank hair out of with strips, whilst intensely crap, twinkly music pours out of speakers in an attempt to soothe those being plucked.

Our attitude towards female body hair is slightly twisted, really. When did it become 'attractive' to be so hairless? Free-and-easy access to porn has only exacerbated this obsession. NO ONE should tell us what we should do with our pubes. If you have a partner that does this, stick your tongue out and blow a firm raspberry in their face.

This goes for all hair, everywhere: under your armpits, coming out of your nostrils, on your arms and legs, on your upper lip, out of your bum, on your toes and around your belly button. Let it be your choice what you do or don't do with your hair – NEVER feel like you HAVE to do anything. Cos quite frankly you DON'T.

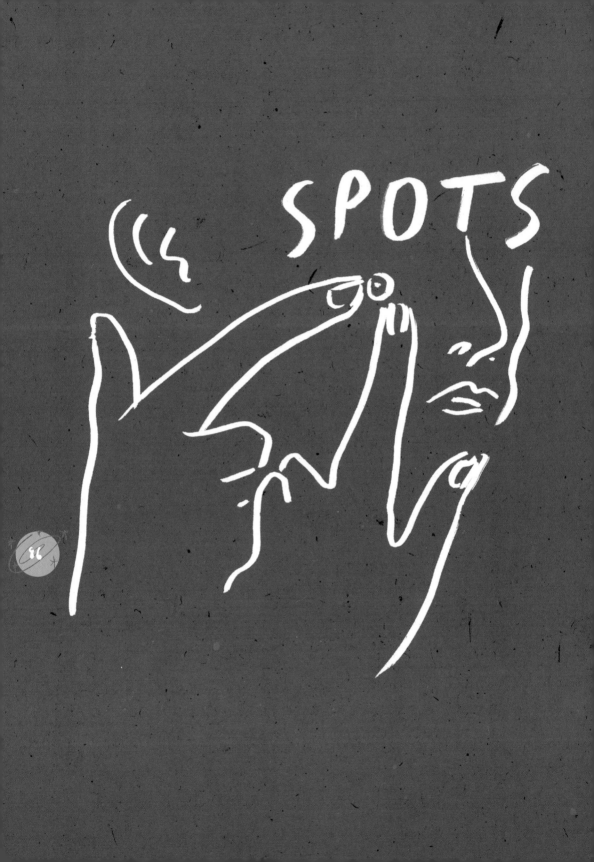

When I made a documentary about acne a few years ago for BBC3, I found myself flooded with emotional memories of the sadness and shame around having spotty skin, especially as a teenager.

I interviewed a young man who had not only had his confidence knocked by his severe acne, but had found it actually physically painful too, especially at night when he was lying on his bed, because he had acne on his back that was incredibly sore. He found it hard to look people in the eye and stooped his head low. He was prepared to do anything to get rid of it, though he had decided against taking what's often the 'last resort' prescribed by doctors and dermatologists – a drug called 'Roaccutane', which is linked to quite a lot of side-effects, from tiredness, to dry lips and even suicidal thoughts. He and his mum saved up for a year to have some private treatment involving light therapy, which in the end worked really well. BUT it wasn't cheap.

I learned a lot from making this doc – the biggest lessons being that there are many, many routes to clear skin. You just have to keep an open mind and not give up, make sure you research whatever you are prescribed (always) and that you read all the information that comes with prescribed drugs. Make decisions for yourself, and try not to get too bogged down. You also have to remember that acne is a universal issue, and that people don't judge you for having spots.

Another key thing to remember – very often, spots and acne are at their worst during the teenage years, and sometimes into your early twenties, but most people eventually grow out of it. Be patient. Keep calm. Things can only get better.

# BODY IMAGE

66 The situation with our bodies is pretty serious. We're sort of supposed to have our body as our product rather than the place we live from, and that's a really damaging concept. 99

Susie Orbach, author of seminal work *Fat is a Feminist Issue*. Her thoughts on women's relationships with their bodies these days are pretty clear.

We are bombarded with an overwhelming amount of images of unattainable bodies every minute of every day. According to recent stats, we check our phones up to 200 times a day on average. If most of that time is spent looking at the ideals we can never live up to, it's gonna be tough for our self-esteem to stay intact.

Body shaming is a complex issue. I'm fully aware that there is an argument for all body shapes, and that not one particular industry is to blame, especially with the swell of online activity adding petrol to the flames. Fitness trends and eating fads that are completely unregulated are reaching insane levels of popularity. How are we honestly supposed to find a balance when it comes to food, exercise and what our bodies should look like when we are bombarded with 'thinspiration', #bodygoals and the perfect thigh gap?

The truth is that some body shapes cannot be achieved unless a person dedicates their entire life to achieving it, monitoring everything that goes into it and denying themselves some of life's most wondrous things – like different types of food – and sacrificing playtime for exercise time. So STOP. Listen to your body. Figure out what makes you feel healthy and wonderful – what food you find delicious and makes you feel happy inside. Find your own way of making your body bend, stretch, flex and work up a sweat (refer to EXERCISE on page 108 for more on this). It's your choice, and nobody else's.

What needs to be celebrated in society, and adored by ourselves and the mainstream media alike, is the HEALTHY body size – which is the body size we are each naturally supposed to be, and is different for all of us.

Take ownership and responsibility for yourself and for the 'brain food' you consume. Be careful about who you follow on Instagram, and check in with yourself to work out how what you're seeing is making you feel. Does it feel good to want a body shape that is difficult to attain . . . or is it hard work, miserable and counter-productive?

## Do you find yourself agreeing with any of the following statements?

I wish I didn't look this way.

I often look at pictures of women's bodies in the media, and it makes me feel bad about my own body.

I find myself constantly researching and thinking of ways to try to look different to how I do now.

If you found yourself answering YES to any of the above, then it is time to actively work on your self-esteem and change some unhealthy online viewing habits.

I once interviewed two girls who told me that together they could spend up to six hours searching the word 'skinny' on Tumblr. It was only when they said that out loud that they realized that it wasn't doing them any good.

Start focusing on the bits of yourself that you do like, the bits that make you feel happy, strong and in control. People talk about eyes being beautiful because they are: go look at yours. They are your two portals to your inner galaxies: full of mermaid-tail blues, greys and greens, all the autumnal magic of brown, hazel and amber. Your eyes are breathtakingly beautiful.

The relentless and futile pursuit of perfection is all around us, and we have to find some way to cope with it, to see our bodies as not just good enough, but COOL AS F*CK! YOUR BODY IS VALUABLE AND REMARKABLE. The minute you accept that no one fits into the 'cookie cutter' of perfect, is the minute you will realize that all bodies are beautiful, including yours.

Personally, I want to live a life of extraordinary adventure, soul-igniting fun times, inquisitiveness and individuality . . . but I want to do it with my healthy, strong, NORMAL body.

As an experiment, I challenged my friends to draw their interpretation of their naked bodies on to an array of nude-(ish – it was way more difficult than I thought to buy the right skin-toned material!)-coloured body suits. I expected people to draw their self-portrait naturalistically, like I did – and I got on with colouring-in and thinking about what I look like with no clothes on. When I turned round, I realized everyone had gone rogue, and alternative body portraits were being created instead.

I loved the symbolism of this: the fact that our bodies can be WHATEVER WE WANT THEM TO BE.

**Anna Hart:** Swirly whirligig boobs and matching bush.

*My body is mine, for feeling, using and enjoying. My body does not exist for other people to look at. Do something with your body that makes you feel strong and capable and free. Don't treat your body like an ornament.*

**Brigitte Aphrodite:** Black lacy cycling shorts, and leaves on her boobs.

*Your body is just a load of cells. When you look in the mirror, don't obsess over the finer details — do a wiggle, just to see if you like the way your clothes swing, check for bogeys and then go.*

**Jessica Jordan-Wrench:** All-seeing, all-knowing eyes for boobs.

*Long walks, short swims and exuberant dancing outshines calorie counting. In so many ways.*

92

**Me:** Chocolate-button-brown nips, and a big proud bush.

*My body usually responds well to its environment. If I am in the gym, it will suddenly, when pushed, be quite strong; my feet didn't ache too much when I trekked up Mount Kenya; and it responds brilliantly to a cuddle.*

**Emma Gibson:** Smiley face for pregnant tummy.

*No one really cares what you look like; they are too busy thinking about how they look themselves.*

**Zezi Ifore:** Bowie-inspired lightning-bolt body contouring.

*Dress sizes in shops are totally meaningless. Try stuff on (ESPECIALLY if buying vintage!), and if you feel mega/cool as hell/fabulous, then get it. Anything less, leave it behind. Greater treasures await!*

**Frances Acquaah:**
#BlackLivesMatter tattoo,
pom-pom, bunny-tail bum.

*Images of perfection are
shoved in our faces at
every possible opportunity,
and I am more self-
conscious than I have ever
been. Everything will
change very quickly. In
all things, embrace the
present. You will blink and
it will be ten years later!*

**Laura Cairney-Keize:**
Purple-star vagina.

*Your body changes
constantly — if you
look after it, it will
look after you.*

**Georgia Lewis-
Anderson:** Psychedelic
purple daisies for
boobs.

*Dress sizes in shops
can be confusing and
totally vary. I'm
actually a different
size on the top and
bottom.*

93

**Amy Redmond:** Rainbow vagina.

*I wish I had known when I
was a teenager that true
happiness comes from within;
that staring in the mirror
won't change anything;
and that wasting your
time, energy and thoughts
on ways to look thinner is
exactly that, a waste.*

**Jessica Thandi Berry:**
Lips on lips.

*The most extraordinary part of my body
isn't a physical thing. I have pretty
vivid and crazy dreams, so the part
of the brain that can dream is pretty
extraordinary to me.*

# SHOW US YOUR BODY STORY

Use the colour code below to show your story.

● has seen me through adventure

● is gentle

● has overcome something

● is strong

● I love this part

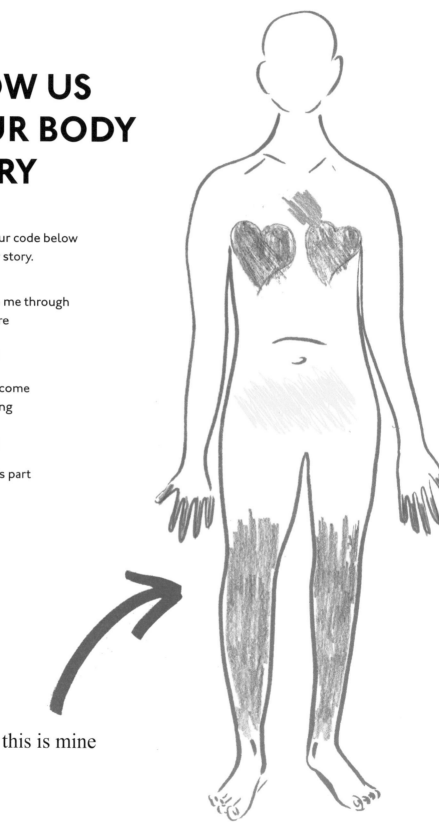

this is mine

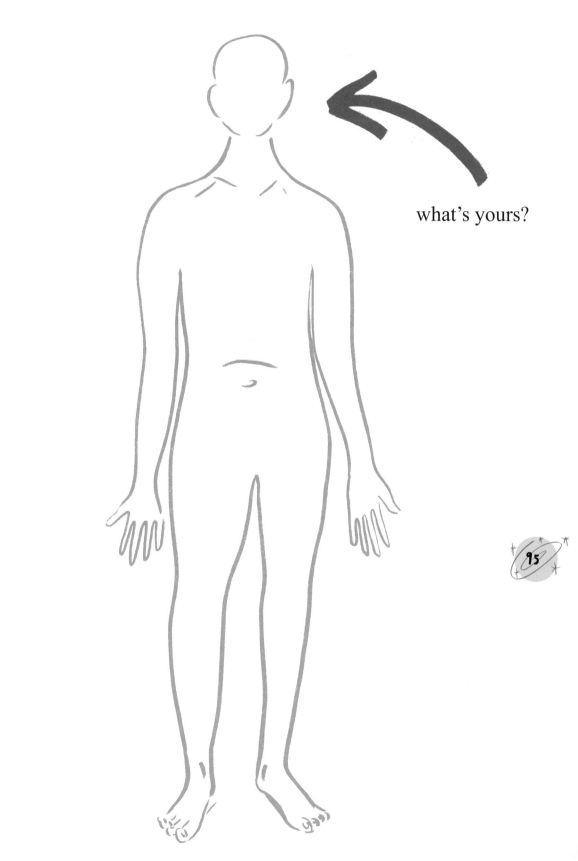

what's yours?

95

## SPANDANGLE THE BITS YOU LOVE

If you like certain parts of your body, then show them off that bit more. It can be any bit: your wrists (get the sparkliest watch); your nose (get a buzz-cut and show off your nose proudly to the world); your calves (roll up your jeans and wear rainbow-coloured socks pulled up); your bum bum (shake it, shake it); your tum tum – no matter the size! Don't be afraid of sunnier climes and the notion of whether you're 'bikini body ready'. Personally, I love a swimming costume – for me, they are (and always will be) so much more fun to wear than a bikini. They stay on when you jump in the water; they protect you more from the sun. Don't get me started on the reasons I love a swimming costume! Well, if you insist . . .

**Reasons I love a swimming costume (the mini manifesto):**

* They make me feel 'held in'. Feeling 'held in' is good. It makes you feel more bendy – and less self-conscious when you want to cartwheel on the beach.

* The leg of a cossie is often more 'realistically' cut for bushes. Yep – PUBIC HAIR AGAIN.

* If you buy a vintage one (do, and give it a boil wash) or one designed like a vintage one (which you can very easily online), you can ACTUALLY feel like a Hollywood star from the 1950s.

* If you look hard enough, you can even get a 'SWIM DRESS' – an actual dress to swim in! One step beyond a swimming costume, it's like a full dress, and in my opinion is the dream – covering your nether regions, swaying with sass as you sashay around the pool.

Having said all that, if you want to wear a bikini and your stomach is not like a washboard, then you're going to look beautiful too. Don't hide your loveliness if you don't want to. Whatever makes you feel good, and comfortable – you do YOU.

COLOUR ME IN!

# CLOTHES

They can give your soul the most fabulous lift.

I love clothes. My eyes are always on stalks for fabric that is bold and that glistens, for opportunities to experiment with colours and patterns that bring bursts of joy, ridiculousness and fun to my soul and stir my imagination. My clothes represent all the things that I'm made of, all the different things that I feel. I like to shop for clothes when I'm in far-flung places, on holidays and trips, so that I have mementos of times when at my happiest that I can wrap around me to keep me warm. I honestly get lost in my own faraway land of contentment when I look at old tank tops, Tropicana-printed pyjama-type trousers and denim (that looks like it's been worn by someone who's rolled around for hours on a chalky moon) in vintage shops. I sometimes wish I could actually eat the shoes they make me so happy – they are like sweets, delicious-looking, big shiny 1970s ones that scream and shout disco and dazzling, platform-defying dance moves.

The only real fashion advice I will give in this book is to flip OPEN the lid on your creativity. Never be frightened to wear whatever and be whoever you want to be. Experience the joy of showing off your identity through clothes. If for you that means following a tribe, a cultural scene, or opting to express yourself through clothes of certain cultural significance . . . then that's cool. If it means wearing all the shades of black and grey, then that's cool too. If it's wanting to wear a ball gown to a BBQ, then do it. The most sublimely dressed are those who look like they love what they are wearing.

# Dressing SEXY

Sexiness is great if that's a look you choose to inhabit. But only if you are happy dressing that way. Ask yourself at least three times before you go out if you are comfortable in what you are wearing. The secret to sexiness is that it doesn't come from showing lots of skin, or wearing a specific outfit or piece of clothing – it comes from CONFIDENCE. Sexiness can be found and achieved in the loosest of loose kaftans that swirls around your body, or a pair of dungarees that makes you skip down the street. Your happiness, your delight, your ease with what you're wearing will be infectious.

**And that is sexy.**

# A Warning on short Shorrrrrrtttttsssssss...

## By Gem

Beware of the teeny weeny, tiny whiny, squeeeeeny little denim shorts,
cos if your front crack could talk
it would go on rants,
it prefers longer pants.
Shorts go up your bum,
make festivals less fun,
hours of camel toe,
the worst fanny foe.
Legs sticking to seats,
no protection from heat,
leave the peach exposers
to the fashion posers.
Just beware of the teeny weeny, tiny whiny little denim shorts.

## Isn't it ironic?

Everyone wants what they don't have, right? Those with gloriously curly hair will spend hours upon hours straightening it. Those with brown hair will dye it bright red, and vice versa. Those with small busts want massive bajongas; but those with massive bajongas long for a smaller bust. Shorties look at tall types with green-eyed envy; but then tall types feel self-conscious and wish to be shorter.

Upon research into the 'ideal body', I heard the following statements:

You've gotta have big boobs.

You've gotta have a big bum.

You've gotta have a tiny waist.

You've gotta have a thigh gap.

When you see these things all together, it's a bit ironic, right? A contradiction. Each body description jumps from one to another, and an overwhelming desire for them all could be damaging. I hardly have to spell this out – as most of us know from our own bodies, or those of our mums, sisters and friends – but women with big bums don't often have tiny waists; women with tiny waists don't often have big boobs; and so on. (I know of course there are exceptions, but let's generalize for a moment.)

Without name-checking certain figures of prominence in popular culture, I'm keen to make one thing clear – those that do somehow have all these features together, those that embody all these 'ideals', have usually gone beyond normal lengths to achieve their body shape: exercising an excessive amount, having teams of people that airbrush or enhance and manipulate the images they put out there of themselves. Some of them have even spent lots of money on surgery. People don't naturally have the shape of Jessica Rabbit – Jessica Rabbit is a cartoon character (google her if you don't know who she is).

Psssst – I do love a fabulous cartoon character! Rastamouse, for example, has impeccable dress sense, and Little My from the Moomins is a badass. Plus, when I'm in a mood, some say I have a likeness to Sarah the Dinosaur in *A Land Before Time* . . . (honestly, google and watch them all immediately if you're not familiar with any of these characters). But I'm fully aware they are not real people; they are just cartoons.

# PERFECT

**THE ONLY MAKE-UP TIP**
>>> if you like make-up, use it as your war paint rather than your 'flaw-covering' paint.

What is 'perfect'?

Perfect [*adjective*]
Having all the required or desirable elements, qualities, or characteristics; as good as it is possible to be.

Examples:
'She strove to be the **perfect** wife.'
'Life certainly isn't **perfect** at the moment.'

Interesting that striving to be the 'perfect' wife and wanting a 'perfect' life are used as examples.

103

## WELL, YOU KNOW WHAT . . . I'M SICK OF PERFECT!

I will never be anybody's perfect anything. What a waste of time to strive to be a 'perfect wife'. I would rather 'strive' to have a fun night out, 'strive' for an endorphin rush from swimming in open waters, 'strive' to travel to as many places on the earth as I can and holiday with all my friends, 'strive' to have a house filled with fun and lovely things to look at, especially sunflowers. But, even if I achieved all those things, my life still wouldn't be 'perfect' – because there's no such thing. In fact, I think the only thing that can be considered 'perfect' is a delicious doughnut, just when you are craving a doughnut more than anything.

# PROTECT YOUR SOUL FROM
## THE FEAR OF IMPERFECTION

Sorry to sound harsh, but I can tell you now it's POINTLESS to fear imperfection. That I can promise you. We are big knotty tangles of ups and downs, triumphs and landslides. It's what makes us human.

No lipstick-painted smile can hide it. No tiny waist, wedding ring, lottery win or grade-A exam result can make someone wholly perfect. The trouble is that we now have the technology and the mindset to make ourselves appear perfect – and, in doing so, we just reinforce the idea that this false sense of 'perfection' is desirable and attainable. Things like bodies, jobs, weddings and other big life situations – they can all look perfect on a screen where they can be so easily exaggerated and filtered and edited. (Think about the last time you used a filter to turn a quite boring social activity into what looked like the most fun thing EVER!) But, more than that, you can actually manipulate your face and body using apps to give yourself the smoothest skin, the boobs you want, legs just a bit longer, eyes just a bit bigger. Read that back. Does it frighten you as much as it frightens me?

#RelationshipGoals    #BodyGoals    #SquadGoals    #HashtagEverything!

This is what I sometimes read as an alternative caption when I look at selfies on social media:

The truth is I haven't eaten breakfast today and I feel tired.

The truth is I worry about my looks all the time.

The truth is, looking back at my last ten Insta pictures, I was having a bad day during at least four of those pics, and I don't really like who I've got my arm round in three.

The truth is I've spent many hours of my life working out how to take the best picture.

The truth is I get lonely.

Nobody's actually perfect. Next time you're feeling shitty when you're comparing yourself to other people, unfollow or unfriend those accounts or profiles that make you feel that way. It's time to work out and break down what is feeding this inner yearning to be PERFECT, and to protect ourselves from the negative influence and sense of misery it leaves us with.

# VANITY CULTURE

So, from every angle we are subjected to a huge amount of pressure to embody what society says is beautiful – earlier pages have established that. The harsh reality is that in some extreme cases girls as young as fourteen are having cosmetic procedures to make their faces more 'beautiful'. It comes back to what we're seeing on social media and TV and the rapidly obsessive selfie culture isn't helping.

These days, we are ALWAYS looking at ourselves. Think about our parents. Back when they were teens, they probs only caught their reflection a few times a day: in the morning when they were brushing their teeth, a few times during the day when heading to the loo and then last thing at night when they brushed their teeth again! Now think of all the pictures you've ever seen of them when they were your age. Think about the grainy warmth of printed film photography, its calmness. Think of their faces in the pictures, not overly self-conscious, just smiling, in the moment – NOT worried about what that picture is going to look like straight away a few minutes before they put it online or send it to a friend. They knew that they had to wait until it was printed to see it. Living in the moment, oblivious and carefree, equals natural beauty. Yes, I have personally taken selfies, of course, but I try not to pay too much mind to the way I look. It's something I've almost trained myself to do – to not scrutinize myself too much, and to try to live in the moment.

I've said it before: some insecurity about how you look is part of life, especially as we are constantly changing – it can be hard to keep up sometimes; it can be awkward. The bad news is that so-called 'solutions' such as fillers, Botox or cosmetic surgery are more readily available and more affordable than ever, and sometimes conducted by less-than-qualified people. It is now considered acceptable for some young people to pay for these procedures. If you are considering having or have become preoccupied with the idea of cosmetic surgery – please think deep in your soul whether it's something you need to be happy.

I once interviewed two cosmetic surgeons for a show I covered on the BBC World Service called *The Conversation*. Nothing was going to stop me from finding out as much as possible from two women who put people under the knife for their jobs – I was fascinated by them. One doctor was working in Colombia, South America, and practised cosmetic surgery, paid for by people who wanted to change something they didn't like about themselves. And the other doctor was working in South Korea, and mainly operated on those who were in need, reconfiguring those born with a deformity or who'd been disfigured by an accident or disease.

Both surgeons talked about the trends in cosmetic surgery in their parts of the world. I found out that in South Korea, women of all ages want more 'Western-shaped' eyes – that is, for their eyes to be made more round than the traditional almond shape. In Colombia, many women want smaller waists and bigger boobs and bums, like Jessica Rabbit (who I mentioned earlier).

The more the surgeons spoke, the more exasperated and sick I felt. I learned that in Colombia women as young as fourteen sometimes have 'surgery' birthday parties, where they would get a new nose. I heard tales of women coming to consultations convinced that their lives would be so much better if only they didn't look the way they did. And I found out how it felt for both surgeons to be asked to operate on their friends and family. Self-hate is a global issue, I thought. How have we got to a place where at the age of fourteen we are prepared to have our bones cracked to reform them, or have fat sucked from our stomachs and thighs just to, supposedly, look better in clothes?

My aim isn't to shame an entire industry, and there is nothing wrong with taking your own kind of pride in how you look, in feeling your type of best. All I know is that I want to beg young women to rid themselves of the maddening insecurity that is at a saddening all-time high, all over the world. All I can keep doing is telling you, reader, that you are so beautiful, I promise you. Beautiful, just the way you are. I am on my knees, begging you to remember this fact. Even if in the past you felt one way, and now you feel another. You were and always will be BEAUTIFUL.

107

# EXERCISE

First of all, exercise is good for us. It just is. It helps to keep our bodies healthy and it protects us from disease. We need to move our butts. That said, exercise can be taken to extremes and become an addiction and it is important to keep perspective on it. Some people are naturally athletic and sporty; some people are more inclined to take it easier. Whatever type you are, go with your natural rhythm, get your heart beating, your blood circulating, but don't obsess about it. That is counter-productive.

My philosophy: move ya body in a way that feels right to you rather than in a way dictated by someone else. We should not be in competition with our friends when it comes to exercise – we know what's right for us; we take our own breaths.

I love to move, whether it is to bend in satisfying lunges, roll my head around in circular motions on the end of my neck like a Jabberwock, or to shake ma tail feather like a Queen Bee doing the 'Waggle' dance. To move is one of the magic things about having a body: it aligns and centres us and creates a kind of euphoria that I adore. I'm all for the endorphins that exercise release – for feeling good in our minds and in our limbs, for feeling happy and strong. But a great body is not one that has been pushed and pummelled and exhausted on a daily basis. A great body is one that zings with health and energy.

The best exercise is that which benefits our minds and our bodies. Our inner fitness motor engine will work better if it is fuelled by a love of taking part in an activity, rather than feeling a pressure to push ourselves unnaturally far and turning what should be fun into obsessional behaviour.

**Stop counting, start dancing.** Constant clocking of calories-to-cardio ratio is a waste of time and, quite frankly, A BORE. It even bores *you*, admit it.

I asked founder of the Equus gym, body-positive, fitness-balancing delight and personal trainer **Nic Addison** her thoughts on reaching a healthy attitude towards exercise:

> It really is simple: my job as a personal trainer is to get more people, more active, more often.
>
> It is important to recognize that activity and movement does not mean hitting the gym four times a week! Any movement will be of benefit to your mind, body and spirit.
>
> It's easy to get confused, overwhelmed and intimidated by hard-hitting media on the subject. HIT (high intensity) workouts, strength training, charcoal smoothies . . .

## LET'S START WITH MOVEMENT

For health benefits – not even fitness or fat loss – we <u>MUST</u> walk for thirty minutes every single day. That's not four times a week, that's not power walking up Everest, it's simply walking at your pace for thirty minutes every single day. Sounds easy? Pop a decent pair of shoes on and start TODAY!

## THEN THERE IS THE 80/20 RULE

Adopt a mindful approach to your food, exercise, sleep, stress choices for eighty per cent of the time and allow for flexibility for the remaining twenty per cent. The 80/20 rule is all about setting realistic goals – accepting that we cannot be perfect, and patting ourselves on the back when we achieve that eighty per cent. Achieving eighty per cent across the board will see rapid, consistent, sustainable body results. I am forever telling my clients that being consistently good at eighty per cent is far better than being inconsistently excellent at a hundred per cent!

80/20%

## PERMISSION

Following the 80/20 rule gives you complete power and the permission to enjoy your life.

The 80/20 rule for me means that for five days of the week I won't have that biscuit with my mid-morning cuppa; I will opt for a sparkling water over the bottle of BrewDog in the fridge; I will ensure protein is in every meal; I will make sure I go to bed at a decent time. For two days of the week I enjoy my curry, have that drink, go to bed a bit later, eat some Maltesers and just basically live guilt-free with a smug smile on my face.

## MOVEMENT FOR RESULTS

ON TOP of our daily thirty minutes of walking for health, when you are seeking results relating to achieving your fitness goals, that's when 'exercise' comes in to play. Exercise that makes your heart pump, your forehead sweaty and your fingers and toes tingly three times a week for a minimum of twenty minutes will see you achieve those results.

Initially it doesn't matter what the mode of exercise is. It's the adherence that is key. So, if you like Zumba, do Zumba. If football is your thing – do that. If you love making loud exercise noises in your lounge to a fitness DVD, do that three times a week, consistently, for a few weeks.

So, chase endorphins by bowling about the park with your mates. Move, stretch, go dancing. BREATHE. Don't get trapped in a spider's web of feeling like you have to try to achieve something just because you've seen it on Instagram. Yes, go to the gym, if that's your thing, but exercise should not have to cost loads of money. If you're going to get a personal trainer, do some research. It's cheaper to share one, for instance. Try something before committing to it. Check your compatibility with it. Not everything is for everyone.

## GEM SAYS!

I'm happiest when a night out involves disco-dancing, twirling, gliding and grooving. Spinning classes to crappy music with the loom of horror stories just ain't my jam: people passing out, or someone with a Britney mic, a wry smile and a rock-hard body screaming at you to go faster. Not for me. I love swimming in cold water that makes me feel tingly and 'screamy' and alive, I like going to my favourite gym in my sparkly leggings, where there is a trainer and long-term friend who knows my body and fitness levels, makes me giggle and lets me put on ole skool garage music and gives me exercises she knows I'll find fun – like throwing a massive heavy bag from one side of the room to the other. I like a stretch-up with Pilates downstairs at my local coffee shop. These things make me feel energized and happy, like I want to buy beautiful flowers in the florist next door when I leave. Exercise is about our all-round health, and should enhance our love of life.

# QUICK EVERYDAY ACTIVITY TIPS

### 1. Get active every day!

You can burn 250kcal more each day increasing incidental movements – walk when on the phone, do housework, even fidgeting will make a difference. Remember, exercise is not expensive and can actually save money! Simple things like washing the car or vacuuming the carpet will get the heart pumping and the muscles working.

### 2. Learn and love the squat!

Every workout should include some kind of squatting movement. A squat is the staple of all great exercise programmes. Bottom line is that making improvements to the way you look and feel starts with the squat.

### 3. Get crawling!

Crawling is massively underrated and is not just for babies! Crawling refines both gross and fine motor skills by strengthening the large and small muscle groups. It is also fantastic for brain stimulation and creating a spike in the heart rate.

### 4. Hit the dance floor!

Dancing can burn 400 calories per hour! So pop on your favourite song and dance around your living room.

# DYNAMIC STRETCH WORKOUT

It's not always about lifting heavy weights or having the best ever workout, beating your personal best! Sometimes we just need to move. Sometimes we just need to breathe and relax. Sometimes we just need to get the blood pumping. This is the workout that will do just that and will take around twenty minutes. The exercises below are suitable for everyone, of any age or fitness ability. No equipment is needed.

## 1.

**To start off.** Complete each move in order only once. Move as quickly or as slowly as you like. This workout is about range of movement rather than repetitions or pace, so take your time and exaggerate every move.

- March on the spot for twenty steps.
- Complete ten shoulder circles: hands touching the shoulders; complete big circles of the elbows.
- Complete ten torso twists: hands touching the elbows; take a wide stance and twist the torso.
- Complete ten knee hugs: raise one knee at a time and hug it into your chest; alternate legs, five on each side.
- Complete ten heel kicks: bring one heel to the buttocks; alternate, ten each side.
- Complete ten toe touches: push a leg out to the side, reach forward and touch the toe. Repeat.
- Complete ten back taps: raise one arm high, bend at the elbow and touch between your shoulder blades with your hand. Alternate and complete ten on each side.

## 2.

**Read on for a more technical, dynamic work-out.** Complete three of each move then move on to the next exercise.

- Stand tall, breathe in and reach both hands as high as you can in the air, shrug the shoulders, lifting your chest and lift up on to your tiptoes.
- Place heels back on the floor, breathe out and bend forward at the hips, taking your hands forward and then down towards your toes, stretching your hamstrings. Take a breath and rise back to standing. Repeat.

- Stand, then crawl forward on to your hands and into a push-up position. Pause then crawl back up to standing. Repeat.
- Stand, then crawl back into a press-up position. Lower your hips to the floor, lift your chest and draw back the shoulders. Lower chest back to the floor. Repeat.
- Lying on the floor, bring your heels towards the buttocks, reach back to grip your feet at the laces and clench buttocks to stretch the front of the thigh. Release the legs back to the floor. Take a breath. Repeat.
- Push your body back up into a push-up position, walk the hands back, place palms on the thighs and push up to stand up.

## 3.

**Now a little slower to finish . . .**

- Complete five shoulder circles: hands touching the shoulders; complete big circles of the elbows.
- Complete five torso twists: hands touching the elbows, take a wide stance and twist the torso.
- Complete five knee hugs: raise one knee at a time and hug it into your chest; alternate legs, five on each side.
- Complete five toe touches: push a leg out to the side, reach forward and touch the toe. Repeat.
- Complete five back taps; raise one arm high, bend at the elbow and touch between your shoulder blades with your hand. Alternate and complete five on each side.

# FOOD, GLORIOUS FOOOOD

Gobble, gobble, gobble. Someone at the top of the advertising food chain is making bucket-loads of cash. Gobble, gobble, gobble. You'd think that the mine of information we can access about what we should and shouldn't eat would make dietary experts out of us all these days. That we'd be sophisticated and highly informed, with superb food and nutrition knowledge.

Unfortunately it's a little more confusing than that, and there's almost too much information, much of it conflicting, and lots of non-qualified people out to make a quick buck by offering 'aspirational foodie lifestyles'. How healthy are these eating plans really? To get a view from a bona fide expert, I talked to Leo Pemberton, a registered dietitian and nutritionist, who works with people and organizations advising on healthy eating and diet. The full interview with Leo is available as an *OPEN* podcast. It's useful. Go listen to it!

There are a couple of trends that do worry me. One would be the clean-eating movement. At first glance, that doesn't appear to be dangerous . . . but it can lead to disordered eating, because if you start to cut out lots of different food groups . . . only go for raw foods instead of cooked foods, for example, or if you're going gluten free, then going vegan, on top of that, suddenly you're left with not very much in your diet, or maybe only vegetables or only one food group. It can spiral.

One of the dangerous things is that if you follow certain bloggers or Instagram stars, they will all have a slightly different ethos . . . It's not necessarily backed up by science; their advice may swing dramatically from what your goals are. Lots of people want to follow a healthy diet for weight loss, and there are lots of ways you can lose weight, but if you're cutting out vitamins and minerals and things like calcium or protein from your diet — especially if you're still growing or you're very active — that's when it becomes dangerous and you can run into deficiencies, for example.

There are some very good people out there who do give sound advice. But on the flipside a lot of personal trainers or fitness gurus will also claim to be nutrition or fitness experts, and the advice that they often give out is either wrong or misleading, or they have their own theories on what is good in terms of nutrition.

One of the issues I have with some food bloggers and personalities out there is sometimes they can be very, very slim, which isn't a problem — lots of people are naturally slimmer. But it's this image and how they portray it with Instagram or certain blogs that make people want to buy into the 'slimness' posed as nutrition. Whereas the reality is it might not be their diet or their lifestyle that has contributed to their look.

115

I think, in general, we have to be very careful when we start following or copying what someone else is doing.

In terms of the link between the trends and the clean-eating movement and anorexia, I don't think the link is incredibly clear yet. However, I'm certainly seeing a lot of people who appear to be suffering from the symptoms of what we've termed orthorexia — cutting out many food groups to the point where that has an effect on everyday life, and duties, and socializing for example. That's certainly something that I'm seeing.

The bottom line should be that you can be a healthy body weight, live a long life, have a healthy skeleton and live a successful life, having a balanced diet including all food groups in your diet.

**"**

## WHAT IS ORTHOREXIA?

**orthorexia** *[noun]*
An obsession with eating foods that one considers healthy.
A medical condition in which the sufferer systematically avoids specific foods that they believe to be harmful.

If you are feeling concerned or confused by your own eating habits, or someone else's, please head to the back of this book, where there is a list of organizations that will be able to offer you specific advice.

# SEX

Let's talk about it. Sex, after all (whether we like it or not), is how we exist. Our bodies and souls are so connected to our relationship with sex and everything that surrounds it: who we love, who we fancy, how we choose to explore those feelings, and the decisions that we and those close to us make when it comes to sex and sexuality.

THE LEGAL BIT

The age of consent for any form of sexual activity is sixteen for both men and women. The age of consent is the same regardless of the gender or sexual orientation of a person and whether the sexual activity is between people of the same or different gender.

It is an offence for anyone to have any sexual activity with a person under the age of sixteen.

It is an offence for a person aged eighteen or over to have any sexual activity with a person under the age of eighteen if the older person holds a position of trust (for example, a teacher or social worker) as such sexual activity is an abuse of the position of trust.

If there was an aisle for 'sex' in the supermarket, it'd be somewhere between the golden syrup and the treacle – all tempting and gloopy. It drip, drips into our brains, confusing us, exciting us, making us giggle. It's a subject that at some point in our lives most of us will experience in some way. But if you are yet to experience it, it can be a daunting, scary, BIG thing.

Sex is personal. Not just because it is an intimate act, but because it is individual to each of us. We are each comfortable with different things, and we each have our own pace. When you're a teenager, it is easy to feel pressured into it – either by other people or by yourself. Sex seems to be all around us, online, on TV, on advertising billboards, on magazine covers. It's easy to feel that everyone is doing it, and doing it right.

But it is up to you, and only you, how you feel about sex. Not what your friends say, or what you may have watched online or in a film. YOU are the keeper of your body and soul, and when it comes to doing it, it needs to be a consensual, respectful act between you and your partner. Consensual sex is not just a physical act; it is an emotional one too. And it has consequences – ranging from feeling vulnerable and strange, to becoming pregnant or contracting an STD. Before you do it, prepare yourself, make sure you are safe. It's so important to explore what we are personally comfortable with and to think it through before we do it. It is ALWAYS one hundred per cent fine to say NO. It is ALWAYS OK to express yourself and say how you feel when it comes to sex. If you don't want to do it for any reason, then under no circumstances do you have to.

Your body is nobody's but yours. Be confident and sure about the person with whom you choose to share it. And always, always, ALWAYS make sure you are feeling safe and comfortable.

Me? I'm continuously confused by sex. My feelings towards sex change all the time. What it is, what it means to me, how much I like it, and what I like about it. It changes depending on who you're with, how you are feeling in your soul, what's going on in your life outside the partnership, how you are feeling about your health and your body at any given time. In essence, I think it's best to just accept that we'll never have all the answers, and just when we think we're crystal clear in our opinions, thoughts, wants and desires . . . they will change again. As long as we are being safe and considering each and every sexual decision we make, then we can control how vulnerable it makes us.

# FIVE THINGS SEX SHOULD BE

1 Within your boundaries, which you have the right to change at any time, according to how you feel.

2 Mutually fun and caring.

3 FULLY CONSENSUAL for everyone involved.

4 With someone you trust and think is great.

5 SAFE.

# FIVE THINGS SEX SHOULDN'T BE

1 Pressured or forced.

2 Uncomfortable or consistently painful.

3 Putting your sexual health at risk.

4 With someone you don't trust.

5 Shared online or with strangers against your wishes or without your knowledge.

# SEXUALITY

Who we are and who we share our love and intimacy with is a decision more personal than nearly anything else in our lives. This doesn't make it any easier if you are feeling confused or you are worried about what people might think of your sexuality.

REMEMBER: do not feel you have to define your sexuality to anyone if you don't want to.

## Personal trainer and presenter Georgie Okell opens up on her experience of coming out.

" The things we tell ourselves can be quite amazing. The stories we create in our own minds. The stories we allow to build and grow and extend so far into and across our consciousness that they begin to obscure what is real.

One of the stories I had created by my second year of university went like this: if everyone finds out you're gay, you're going to have to leave. Leave this uni, leave this town, start again. How embarrassing. How utterly inconvenient. Best to keep that information under wraps. Better to have cool friends and be popular and date boys you don't fancy just so you look the part. Better, even, to have a girlfriend you keep secret, who you meet up with late at night, whose calls you don't answer when you're with friends. Who you are utterly in love with but ashamed to be seen with, in case anyone figures out the terrible truth.

I'd known for ages, of course. I remember kissing a girl at fourteen and feeling the entire world melt around us, like nothing else existed. My brain was all fireworks and explosions; my heart practically bursting out of my chest. Despite that, I deemed those feelings undesirable. I decided maybe it might be best and sensible if I ignored them and definitely didn't talk about them. I hoped, actually, that they might go away and I'd never have to feel those wonderful feels about a girl ever again.

Thankfully, love and lust don't work like that. The fireworks kept coming back, refusing to be ignored into submission. So around the age of nineteen, I began to acknowledge them, begrudgingly. I certainly didn't accept them, though, nor did I think it wise to share how I felt with anyone lest people look at me differently. Heaven forbid. What other people thought about me was the single most important thing in the world and, as long as I continued to fit in, I'd be just fine.

My coming-out story is underwhelming. Get ready: one night at university in my second year, I was stood outside a house party with my two (straight) best friends, and they said, 'Georgie, we know you have a girlfriend. We don't care.' Just like that. That was the huge coming-out moment I had dreaded and

feared. Over in an instant. My internal relief and joy was much, much bigger than the moment itself, and I felt an overwhelming sense of everything shifting. In that one moment, I knew I was on the path to opening up and being myself. That path hasn't always been easy or comfortable. There have been bumps in the road, difficult periods with my family and their acknowledgment of my sexuality. Letters I wrote which were met with gaping silence from those not willing to hear what I was telling them. It has taken me the best part of a decade to be truly, truly comfortable with being an out-and-proud gay woman who can talk about it, write about it, shout about it from the rooftops.

I knew that for sure when I finally started to stand up for myself and not allow other people to decide how I was portrayed in the public sphere. I remember particularly presenting a television show in the US a couple of years ago and being told to walk differently, talk differently, grow my hair, wear more make-up, talk about male pop stars in a way that might suggest I fancied them. I declined to do any of the above. I look how I look. I feel how I feel. I love who I love. Take it or leave it.

Being different certainly tests our sense of self, to step out of what is easy and acceptable and start to shape and define ourselves as an individual — it's scary. But taking ownership of all that makes us wholly and truly ourselves. It's the single most important thing we can do. To ignore or conceal any aspect of who we really, truly are, to live uncomfortably in a skin that doesn't quite fit instead of comfortably in our own is weirdly easy,

but it's also a waste. A waste of all the little things that make you you.

I'm lucky — the bumpy road I've stumbled along for the past decade is nothing compared to the mountains I know some have climbed just to be able to have their sexuality acknowledged. Honesty and openness require bravery, but if there is one thing in life worth fighting for it is the ability to be completely ourselves, and to love genuinely and wholeheartedly. Stories are great, but the truth is always greater.

**"**

123

# GENDER AND SEXUALITY

It's important that we equip ourselves with the tools of communication when it comes to the distinct issues of gender, sexual orientation and sexuality. It is powerful and special to be able to talk about these things. It enables us to try to understand ourselves and those around us.

## Glossary of terms and definitions for the realms of gender and sexuality

Provided by Suran Dickson, founder of Diversity Role Models (DRM). DRM tackles bullying related to gender and sexuality and encourages critical thinking by taking positive role models into schools.

**A**

**Ally:** a (typically) straight and/or cisgender person who supports members of the LGBTQ (lesbian, gay, bisexual, transsexual and queer) community .

**B**

**Asexual:** someone who does not experience sexual attraction

**Biphobia:** the fear or dislike of someone who identifies as bisexual.

**Bisexual or bi:** refers to a person who has an emotional and/or sexual orientation towards more than one gender.

**C**

**Cisgender or cis:** a person whose gender identity is the same as the sex they were assigned at birth. 'Non-trans' is also used by some people.

**Coming out:** when a person first tells someone/others about their identity.

**D**

**Deadnaming:** calling someone by their birth name after they have changed their name. This term is often associated with transexual people who have changed their name as part of their transition.

**G**

**Gay:** refers to a man who has an emotional, romantic and/or sexual orientation towards men. Also a generic term for lesbian and gay sexuality – some women define themselves as gay rather than lesbian.

**Gender dysphoria:** when a person experiences discomfort or distress because there is a mismatch between their sex assigned at birth and their gender identity. This is also the clinical diagnosis for someone who doesn't feel comfortable with the gender they were born with.

**Gender identity:** a person's internal sense of their own gender, whether male, female or something else (see 'non-binary' below).

**Gender queer:** someone who doesn't identify with traditional binary gender roles, and instead identifies as neither, both, or a combination of them.

**Gender reassignment:** another way of describing a person's transition. To undergo gender reassignment usually means to undergo some sort of medical intervention, but it can also mean changing names, pronouns, dressing differently and living in their self-identified gender. Gender reassignment is protected by the Equality Act 2010.

**Gender Recognition Certificate (GRC):** this enables trans people to be legally recognized in their self-identified gender and to be issued with a new birth certificate. Not all trans people will apply for a GRC, and you have to be over eighteen to apply. You do not need a GRC to change your gender at work or to legally change your gender on other documents such as your passport.

**Gender stereotypes:** the ways that we expect people to behave in society according to their gender, or what is commonly accepted as 'normal' for someone of that gender.

**Gender variant:** someone who does not conform to the gender roles and behaviours assigned to them at birth. This is often used in relation to children or young people.

**H** **Heterosexual/straight:** refers to a person who has an emotional, romantic and/or sexual orientation towards people of the opposite gender.

**Homophobia:** the fear or dislike of someone who identifies as lesbian or gay.

**Homosexual:** this might be considered a more clinical term used to describe someone who has an emotional romantic and/or sexual orientation towards someone of the same gender. The term 'gay' is now more generally used.

**I** **Intersex:** describes a person who may have the biological attributes of both sexes or whose biological attributes do not fit with societal assumptions about what constitutes male or female. Intersex people can identify as male, female or non-binary.

**L** **Lesbian:** refers to a woman who has an emotional, romantic and/or sexual orientation towards women.

**LGBTQ:** the acronym for lesbian, gay, bi and trans and queer.

**N** **Non-binary:** an umbrella term for a person who does not identify as male or female.

**O** **Outed:** when a lesbian, gay, bi or trans person's sexual orientation or gender identity is disclosed to someone else without their consent.

**P** **Pansexual:** refers to a person who is not limited in sexual choice with regard to biological sex, gender or gender identity.

**Pronoun:** words we use to refer to people's gender in conversation – for example, 'he' or 'she'. Some people may prefer others to refer to them in gender-neutral language, and use pronouns such as 'they'/'their' and 'ze'/'zir'.

**Queer:** in the past, considered a derogatory term for LGBTQ individuals. The term has now been reclaimed by LGBTQ young people in particular who don't identify with traditional categories around gender identity and sexual orientation, but is still viewed to be derogatory by some.

**Questioning:** the process of exploring your own sexual orientation and/or gender identity.

**Sex:** assigned to a person on the basis of primary sex characteristics (genitalia) and reproductive functions. Sometimes the terms 'sex' and 'gender' are interchanged to mean 'male' or 'female'.

**Sexual orientation:** a person's emotional, romantic and/or sexual attraction to another person.

**Trans:** an umbrella term to describe people whose gender is not the same as, or does not sit comfortably with, the sex they were assigned at birth. Trans people may describe themselves using one or more of a wide variety of terms, including (but not limited to) transgender, cross-dresser, non-binary, genderqueer (GQ).

**Transgender man:** a term used to describe someone who is assigned female gender at birth, but identifies and lives as a man. This may be shortened to trans man, or FTM, an abbreviation for female-to-male.

**Transgender woman:** a term used to describe someone who is assigned male gender at birth, but identifies and lives as a woman. This may be shortened to trans woman, or MTF, an abbreviation for male-to-female.

**Transitioning:** the steps a trans person may take to live in the gender with which they identify. Each person's transition will involve different things. For some this involves medical intervention, such as hormone therapy and surgeries, but not all trans people want or are able to have this. Transitioning also might involve things such as telling friends and family, dressing differently and changing official documents.

**Transphobia:** the fear or dislike of someone who identifies as trans.

**Transsexual:** this was used in the past as a more clinical term (similarly to *homosexual*) to refer to someone who transitioned to live in the 'opposite' gender to the one assigned at birth. This term is still used by some, although many people prefer the term 'trans' or 'transgender'.

So, who are you? In your heart, what is your identity? Imagine feeling that you were born in the wrong body. Perhaps you are feeling that way and you're finding it hard to find someone to connect to? There is a supportive movement out there for those looking to navigate the complicated subject of gender.

I am in awe of the transgender community, and the bravery and commitment of those transforming their lives. In order to truly understand what it's like to be trans, it's important to talk about it and realize that's it wrong to 'freakify' anyone on the planet – it's time to humanize instead.

I interviewed the immensely clever writer **Juno Dawson**, a transgender woman, who was happy to open up on the subject for *Open*.

**GC:** **Do you still feel that there's a problem when it comes to representation of different sorts of people, representing different stories in the media in general? Not just in literature, but when you watch the telly, when you go to the cinema . . .**

**JD:** Yeah, I think it's getting better, I'll definitely say that. And we have to bear in mind that as an LGBT community we are looking at about five per cent of the population. So I guess you'd expect about five per cent of the people you see on the telly and in films to be from the LGBT community . . . I don't think we're there yet. Although we're getting better.

I think reality TV completely changed representation on television of minority groups, in that drama and scripted drama was so white and so straight at the time, but then all of a sudden *Big Brother* started, and clearly they were looking to cast a diverse group. Nadia was, I guess, the first trans woman to feature significantly on British television, and that was now over a decade ago. Really, now, when you look at *EastEnders*, *Coronation Street*, *Hollyoaks*, they are fairly diverse. I think actually if anyone's got a real problem it's Hollywood, where we are still seeing the same ten white heterosexual cisgender actors playing all the roles.

**GC:** How are we able to feel more comfortable with chatting about the normalization of LGBT representation?

**JD:** It's tough because you constantly get two lots of cries: the sort of man-babies — if you look at the response to *Ghostbusters* for example — 'Oh, there's a gay agenda. There's a trans agenda.' Or, similarly, you get people from within the community saying it's tokenism. So it's really hard to win. But I think being able to humanize groups is really important. We have to get away from this idea that minority groups are a mass of people who will eat and speak exactly the same. Young people seem much more able to take people as individuals . . . It's ridiculous to say that all Muslim people are the same, or that all trans people are the same, or that all gay people are the same. So I think the positive effect of better representation is it humanizes minority groups more, hopefully.

**GC:** If you're not trans, but trying to talk about it, it's easy to become fearful of saying the wrong words – calling someone who was a he and now a she, 'he', or vice versa, or not knowing whether to say 'transsexual' or 'transgender', and so on. There are so many different tiers of the unknown for lots of people talking about this sensitive issue, and it does make me worry that it stops people from talking in the first place, and everybody just feels awkward.

**JD:** I'm increasingly aware that we have to be able to have conversations, even if they're difficult. I think one of the downsides of social media has been how reactive and angry we can be. I don't think that trans people should have to debate their existence. I've just, this very week, written an article which is 'The Dos and Don'ts of Asking Trans People Questions'. It's interesting because no white, straight, cisgender man is having to answer questions about what it's like to be a white, straight, cisgender man. But trans representation and trans visibility is so new, and if I'm willing to be out there as a trans woman I am up for answering questions.

You've just got to keep it polite and keep it sane. Would you be asking about your gran's genitals? Would you be asking your gran, 'Do you still sleep with men, or do you sleep with women? What surgeries will you have?' If people come to you with sane questions, even if it's a misconception — like a really common one is, 'Did you used to be a drag queen?' — I'm like, 'Well, no, but I will now explain to you the difference between a performance drag artist and me: the drag artist is being paid. I am not being paid every day to dress like this.'

**GC:** How different is life as Juno in comparison to James? What does the world look like now? Do you face different things day to day, or is it quite similar – you just feel more naturally aligned?

**JD:** Alignment's a really good word. It's funny because in a spiritual — I hate the word 'spiritual' — kind of inner-world way, everything feels very calm and feels very right. I make a lot more sense; my relationships make a lot more sense. Though on a practical level things are a lot harder right now. It's a lot harder to be a woman — you have pressure to look a certain way, to make a lot more effort. I have to get up earlier to get ready, make extra time for leg shaving, extra time for armpit shaving, all of those practical issues that come along with being a woman that I think cisgender women have been doing so long — since they were twelve/thirteen — that actually they forget it's bullshit, and they forget that men are not doing this. So on a practical level it's harder — people stare and people mutter about me, people point me out, people say, 'Oh, that's a man.' I've made things a bit harder for myself, but spiritually I feel better than I've ever felt, and things make a lot more sense.

**GC:** When trying to understand the trans experience more broadly, it's important to remember that everyone's different, right?

**JD:** There are as many ways to be transgender as there are trans people. I am what the kids would call 'binary transgender': I was born physically male, but now I am one hundred per cent convinced I am a woman; I've always been a woman. I want to be called 'she'. My passport now says I'm a woman; my birth certificate will eventually say I'm a woman. For some people it's not that easy — they prefer 'non-binary' or 'gender queer', or 'gender fluid'. But I think the advice that I would give, and I give this advice to young adults who write to me, is be patient, because these things really do take time. There really isn't a rush.

Also, I would say, as pure practical advice (although this is just advice for the UK), do get yourself on a waiting list, because actually waiting lists are so long that that's your thinking time. So I'd almost doubled up on thinking space, because I did two years of thinking time before I even got on a waiting list. Just don't rush things. That's good advice for dealing with your family as well; just because you've been thinking about this for a year and a half, you can't dump it on your parents and expect them to be fine with it in a fortnight.

There is no quick way to transition. I think I've had to learn patience — I was very impatient. And I would say that if you're going to start thinking about gender transition in any regard, really, it's to start thinking about patience first, and understanding that you are in it for the long haul. Because another one of those slightly daft questions that trans people get asked all the time is, 'When will you be finished?' — and actually you're never finished. You're not baking a cake; you're going to be living with your gender identity until you die. So getting patience from day one isn't bad advice, I don't think.

Also, and I think this will chime with younger readers, it doesn't need to be a big deal. When I was in my early twenties, I was in a band — who wasn't? — an electro-punk band, and looking back there was a real trans element to it. I was wearing fur coats, leather pants, stockings and suspenders, and it was pure performance — I wasn't going to Tesco like that. When I look at younger people now, there's more of an element of experimenting with gender — 'Yeah, I'm a girl, but I can wear a suit if I want, I can wear a bowler hat if I want, it's just me playing with fashion, it's me playing with my identity, and it's not permanent.'

That's the other thing with gender — you're not carving it in stone. It is a very sort of hysterical way of looking at transgenderism to think, 'Oh my God, it's this irreversible change. Last week she decided she was trans, so now she's in hospital having surgery.' It really doesn't work like that. I was really proud of Eddie Izzard when he said, 'I'm transgender' — because of course he is — he's playing with hair, clothes and make-up, which is 'gender'. So the word 'transsexual' has weirdly gone out of fashion, but I'm really proud to be a transsexual in that I am, through various medical interventions, now seeking to change my sex.

**GC:** How did your parents take it?

**JD:** Yeah they were good, but they weren't good overnight. I would say there was a definite period where I think my mum in particular thought I was putting myself through hardship, and exposing myself to danger. And, statistically, she is right. I am more vulnerable as a trans woman than I was as a gay man — but then you can only panic for so long. The real surprise was my dad . . . Given that I've not had a great relationship with him, I thought this could be the end. But actually it's made our relationship better, and I think that was because he was trying to make a relationship happen with a son, and he never really had a son . . . He's always got on much better with my sister, because I think he understood how to make a father—daughter relationship work, and now he's just acquired another daughter. So actually we've been getting along better than we have in a really long time. All's well that ends well.

When you're dealing with a relationship with a parent, it feels like there's a lot on the line, like you're really gambling with something special, but it did have to be done. It felt a bit like going to the gallows or something — I got the train up from Leeds and I was like [groans]. I think again it's very much about patience and understanding. As much as you're like, 'Ugh, why can't you be fine with this?' you owe them some time as well, because you've had a lot of time.

**GC:** Do you have any good advice in terms of people to seek out, to google, that have really great opinions or really great experiences on being trans?

**JD:** There's Gendered Intelligence — Gendered Intelligence is a wonderful charity who support both trans people and their parents. There's Mermaids, another charity who particularly support the parents of trans young people. In terms of my personal role models, for me it was about finding trans people who were my age, I think, more than anything. I was looking up to people like Paris Lees, Andreja Pejić, and I read Juliet Jacques's memoir, which is called *Trans: A Memoir*, which is brilliant. So it's about sort of finding people that chime with you, because there isn't one way to be trans. So not all trans people will necessarily inspire you. I disagree with most of what Caitlyn Jenner says, but I'm still very relieved she exists, because she puts her trans views on a platform that we wouldn't have had otherwise. So I don't agree with her on a political level, but at the same time I really respect everything she's done in terms of being so out there and so open about her gender.

**GC:** **Do you think the internet has elevated the trans rights movement?**

**JD:** Now we've all become sort of experts — the internet has very much democratized freedom of speech in that we all have the same platform now. Before it was the media — the media was in charge of picking people out and saying, 'Her face fits,' or, 'His face fits, so we'll get that person on TV,' and they were very much selected. One of the things I like about the internet is that it has, by default, become more diverse, because we choose who we want to listen to.

But the problem is it's about filtering in or out those people that we think we relate to, I guess, and understanding that a lot of the time these experts that we're seeing on the internet don't necessarily have any

133

qualifications whatsoever. I guess it's about finding those people whose beliefs, politics, faith, most align with yours. But I'm also a big, big believer in 'Turn the computer off and go walk in nature' — you have to have real conversations, and you have to have conversations with people who don't agree with one hundred per cent of the things you say, because if you're in an echo chamber you're not going to be changing anybody's hearts or minds. That's the danger with the internet — because we can select just what we want to hear, and we can convince ourselves that this is the world we're living in. Almost, it's become virtual reality. You have to actually go out and live in the world, with all its problems, with its homophobia and transphobia and racism, otherwise you're living inside a palace of your own creation, and I don't think it's healthy.

**GC:** **What would you say to those who inflict prejudice on the LGBT community?**

**JD:** There have always been transgender people; there have always been LGBT people; there have always been women; there have always been people who are trying to hark back to this 'golden age' that didn't really exist. We're not trying to take anything away from white, cisgender, heterosexual men. I don't want them to lose rights — we're just asking for the same rights. You're not under attack; we're just catching up.

134

# SEXUAL HEALTH

135

# If we're gonna do it, let's do it healthily

Through working on a campaign called When It's On, It's On with Durex (the condom brand), I discovered an alarming new attitude when it comes to our sexual health. A kind of 'invincibility culture' has emerged amongst some young people, and their attitude towards sexually transmitted infections has changed dramatically, stopping many of them from taking the right precautions when it comes to having safe sex. Shockingly, forty per cent of sexually active teens admitted to having sex with more than one person WITHOUT A CONDOM.

Increasingly, young people seem to have the idea that most STIs, such as chlamydia, just aren't that serious and can easily be cleared up with a 'pill'. Even more worrying, almost half of those surveyed said that contracting HIV isn't something that would happen to them or any of their friends. Meanwhile, the numbers of young people catching STIs is on the UP.* You do the maths!

On the bright side, the survey also found that whilst over a third of guys in straight, sexually active couples will sometimes try to get away with not using a condom, loads of others actually say it's a turn on when a woman has the confidence to insist on it, in the heat of the moment. Unsafe sex needs to be a deal breaker!

*VIMN Ad & Brand Solutions Insight with Tapestry Research. Base: 1,641; P16-24.
Winkle Toplines Report, 2015. Beliefs, Insight & Reason-to-Believe screener in the UK, France and Italy. P11.

Yes, there is lots out there in the way of birth control, but the only effective way of preventing pregnancy AND STIs is by arming yourself with things that you can buy easily from a chemist, or a corner shop, a twenty-four-hour petrol station, or even a nightclub: CONDOMS. And yet there is still a needless self-conscious attitude towards getting hold of these marvels.

It seems it's not just teens who are too embarrassed to talk about condoms – or to find out where they can get them for free – even grown-ups have given up on talking to young people about safe sex. Perhaps our growing culture of sexualization amongst teens and increasingly easy access to porn terrifies the grown-ups so much they don't want to break it down and chat about the basics.

This means that everyone is kind of walking around in a horny fog, googling more and more info rather than verbalizing, shooting the breeze or asking trusted experts for the facts.

This time round, I'm begging you to sit up and listen. The fact is that the I-just-use-the-pull-out technique nonsense approach to sex means STIs are on the up. Yep. Gremlins are trying to party on our privates. I know – I sound like a bonkers supply teacher in a sex-ed lesson, but it's true . . . We need to inspire a more positive and confident approach towards safe sex. Fill your back pockets with rubbers.

Whenever I ask anyone of school age about what sex education they receive, I'm alarmed to nearly ALWAYS hear that the sex education in their school is pretty non-connective or non-existent. Where is education going wrong?

# WHAT DO THE EXPERTS SAY?

For thirteen years, Kelly Abbot worked in a pupil referral unit with vulnerable young people in Years 10 and 11, so aged fifteen to sixteen, most of whom were from socially excluded families. Kelly's focus was on sexual health and relationships.

You have to . . . break down those barriers . . . It's not like I was teaching anyone how to do sexual acts. But you cannot turn a blind eye to the fact that we know some young people are already engaging in intimacy, whether it's giving 'hand jobs' or 'blowjobs' or whatever, to full-blown sex. My approach was to desensitize. I'd say, 'You tell me every word that you know for your privates, and then write them up on the whiteboard. There were things I'd never even heard of. I can't go into a classroom and say, 'This is the vagina, these are the labia, and this is the penis.' Some kids don't know what the labia are.

What should sex be taught as? It should be taught as a physical, intimate connection between two people who are emotionally able to deal with the energy that sex generates. We all get to an age when you get tingling sensations — that's human nature. But if you're having those tinglings in your pants, and no one is giving you information at home — like a lot of the young people I was teaching — then some seek sexual contact from their peers. Schools and parents need to be aware of this and the fact that there is the wrong self-education happening out there. What young people aren't getting in schools they are trying to find online instead, a lot of it via porn, which is not a true reflection of real sex whatsoever.

# CONTRACEPTION

If you are under the age of eighteen and are thinking of becoming sexually active, then you need to have a conversation with your GP or local sexual health clinic to discuss how to protect yourself. Your doctor can advise on the right kind of contraception for you, and if necessary talk about any issues around each method and why you need it.

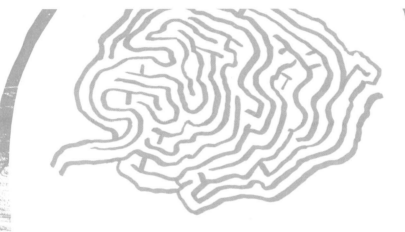

## NAVIGATING THE MIND BOGGLE OF SAFE SEX

I'm gonna start with the fact that the only method of contraception that protects you against nearly all sexually transmitted infections and unwanted pregnancy is a CONDOM. (FYI: if used correctly and consistently it is ninety-eight per cent effective at protecting against unwanted pregnancy, HIV and AIDS, gonorrhoea and chlamydia – definitions on pages 145–6). Yep, a good old, trusty 'rubber johnny', sheath or 'French letter' as your granny might call it (a term that originates from the seventeenth century) or perhaps 'penis hat' as they are sometimes described in Nigeria, or 'love and necessity' in South Korea, or 'safety tool' in Hungary.

(See more detailed benefits on 'penis hats' on pages 136–7.)

*I'm for a condom above anything. It's got yer back from many perspectives.*

**When it comes to heading to the sexual health clinic or going to speak to your GP about contraception, speak UP.** Ask doctors questions. Remember, they **DO NOT JUDGE** their patients, and see many, many, many different people, each with a different story.

## LET'S GET REAL

It goes without saying that nobody's up for an 'unwanted' pregnancy. So there are lots of ways to prevent getting preggo, though the pill and condoms are the most popular, other methods are referred to as contraception too. It's important to know all your options and choose the one that is right for you.

## WHICH KIND OF CONTRACEPTION SHOULD I USE?

There are fifteen different methods of 'birth control' contraception currently available in the UK. The type that works best for you will depend on your health and circumstances, and some are more effective than others. The most widely used forms of contraception in the UK are condoms, followed by the contraceptive pill.

We asked the **Brook Advisory Centre** to provide us with definitions of the types available to younger people:

- **Long active reversible contraceptives** – they do what it says, they last a long time once they are inserted (so you can forget about them) and when you want to get pregnant or stop using them you can get them removed. They are the most effective methods of contraception – over ninety-nine per cent effective – and they include:

    - **Contraceptive implant**

    - **Intra-uterine system, or IUS**

    - **Intra-uterine device or IUD**

    - **Contraceptive injection**

There are other types of contraceptive methods that you need to remember when to take or use. These include:

- **Combined contraceptive pill**

- **Progesterone-only contraceptive pill**

- **Contraceptive patch**

- **Vaginal ring**

- **Male condom**

- **Female condom**

- **Diaphragm**

- **Cap**

**Important** **Forgetting to take or use these methods is a common reason for them failing to protect against pregnancy.**

**Note that if you are taking one form of contraception you can double up by wearing a condom. And, I REPEAT, the ONLY thing that can protect you from a number of STIs is a CONDOM.**

# AMAZING!!

The good news is that there is a scheme that gives out free condoms to those aged thirteen to twenty-four. QUICK, go type 'free condoms' into Google and you will find your local scheme. There you can type in your postcode and it'll tell you how you can get yours. There really is NO excuse not to take advantage of this!

**NO NAMES. NO JUDGEMENTS. NO WORRIES.**

If you have had unprotected sex (that is sex without using contraception) or think that your contraception might have failed, you can use **emergency contraception**. There are different options:

- **Emergency contraceptive pill**. There are two different types:

> 1) Levonorgestrel (Levonelle) can be taken within taken three days (seventy-two hours) after unprotected sex

> 2) Ulipristal Acetate (ellaOne) can be taken five days (120 hours) after unprotected sex.

> These methods will be more effective the sooner they are taken after unprotected sex.

- **Emergency intra-uterine device** (IUD). A small plastic and copper device that can be fitted in your uterus up to five days (120 hours) after unprotected sex. You can choose to keep using the IUD as your regular method of contraception or get it removed during your next period.

There are some brilliant expert websites that will tell you more about contraception, including the **Brook Advisory Centre** mentioned previously and also the ever flabbergastingly amazing **NHS** and the **Family Planning Association**. I don't say it lightly when I say advice is essential when you start having sex. It is some of the most important information you will ever learn.

Young people's contraceptive clinics via the NHS are also a great place to seek unbiased support and do a pregnancy test if there is a worry. A pregnancy test is usually accurate three weeks after the last time you had unprotected sex.

## YOU'VE GOT OPTIONS

If you are pregnant and if you are less than twenty-four weeks pregnant (a doctor can tell you how far along you are) there are three options available to you, and you have the right to choose any one of them:

- Continuing the pregnancy and raising the child
- Continuing the pregnancy and placing the child for adoption
- Ending the pregnancy by having an abortion

# ABORTION

Abortion is the medical process of ending a pregnancy – and is also known as a termination. A pregnancy is ended either by taking medication, or having a minor surgical procedure; this often depends on how far along in your pregnancy you are. Most abortions in England, Wales and Scotland are carried out before twenty-four weeks of pregnancy (calculated from the first day of your last period). They can be carried out after twenty-four weeks in certain circumstances, but they are simpler and safer the earlier they are carried out. Abortion is not legal in the Republic of Ireland or Northern Ireland except in specific situations, where the life of the mother is in danger, for example.

Unwanted pregnancy is definitely something you need to be aware of. One in three women in the UK will have an abortion by the time they are forty-five years old. Though teenage pregnancy has been significantly reduced over the past decade, there is some risk of pregnancy even if you haven't started your periods yet, and sex just once can lead to a pregnancy if no contraception is used.

If you do become pregnant and it is not planned or wanted, your GP and sexual health/ abortion clinics are there to help you deal with your situation and talk through the choices with you to help you decide whether or not to have an abortion.

**Where can I go if I am thinking of or want an abortion?**
You can get help in deciding on whether to have an abortion by contacting:

> The British Pregnancy Advisory Service (BPAS)
>
> Marie Stopes UK
>
> The National Unplanned Pregnancy Advisory Service (NUPAS)
>
> A contraception or family planning clinic, sexual health clinic or genitourinary
> medicine clinic
>
> Your doctor and ask for a referral

**Where is the abortion performed and how long do I have to wait for an appointment?**
Abortions can only be carried out in an NHS hospital or a licensed clinic – nowhere else.

Waiting times vary, but you shouldn't have to wait more than two weeks for your initial

143

appointment to discuss having an abortion. Abortions can also be performed in private licensed clinics, and your doctor can refer you to one if you choose to pay for an abortion.

**Can I get an abortion at any time during my pregnancy?**
It is legal to have an abortion up to twenty-four weeks into a pregnancy in the UK. After this date there must be very specific circumstances, such as danger to the mother's life. In Northern Ireland, where certain situations allow for a legal abortion, it must be carried out before nine weeks and four days gestation.

**How can I tell how many weeks pregnant I am?**
Your doctor will ask you when the first day of your last period was and then calculate from that day. You will also need an ultrasound scan to confirm the exact date. This is particularly important if you have irregular periods, and these happen for lots of reasons – some people can even get pregnant without having a period as they may still ovulate (produce an egg) before a first period happens. And also things like exam stress can make periods irregular.

**What if I am confused and don't know whether I want an abortion?**
The decision to have an abortion is yours and yours alone: only you can make it. But when you seek help you will be told of your options (one of which is going through with your pregnancy) and offered impartial counselling and support to help you decide. It is also important, if you feel that you can, to talk to your parents who will help you think it through. It's one of the most important decisions you will ever make and may well be an emotionally difficult time too. Your family and people who love you are often invaluable in providing support, but if you don't feel you can talk to your parents – if you have an unstable or difficult relationship with them, for example – then seek out trusted friends and other adults, including your local GP or practice nurse. You should not feel in any way pressured into having an abortion or be made to feel ashamed or guilty by anyone.

# STIs

**OH**, and apologies in advance, but this is what we're waging war on by doing our best to keep safe and by using a condom.

You may think that you don't need to worry about sexually transmitted infections, but you do: never be casual about sexual health. Do ask your partner questions about their sexual history and always make sure you're as safe as you can be. An STI, or sexually transmitted infection, is basically any kind of bacterial or viral infection that can be passed on through unprotected sexual contact. It doesn't matter how many times you've had sex or how many partners you've had; anyone can get an STI.

Pay attention to your body and do get anything that is unusual for you checked out, especially if it itches, has come up in a rash or there is unusual discharge. If you don't want to go to your GP – though they have seen everything and will keep it confidential – there are lots of walk-in clinics that you can go to. It is common to feel nervous about getting tested but don't worry – most infections are easily treated. You can find out more information at the Brook Advisory website: www.brook.org.uk

## CHLAMYDIA

The most common bacterial STI is chlamydia. Up to fifty pre cent of girls with chlamydia don't have any symptoms but if left untreated it can have serious consequences, such as pelvic inflammatory disease (PID) and infertility, which means it is important for young people to get tested if they have had unprotected sex, and by that I mean if a condom has not been used. From recent statistics, chlamydia is found in around three per cent of both males and females aged sixteen to twenty-four. Chlamydia is treatable with antibiotics, and it is easy to get tested at your local GP surgery or at a sexual health clinic.

## GENITAL HERPES

Genital herpes is a common infection caused by the herpes simplex virus (HSV). It causes painful blisters on the genitals and the surrounding areas. It is a chronic – long term – condition. It will remain in your body and intermittently become activated – up to four or five times a year in the first two years after infection, though over time it will become less frequent, and less severe.

## GONORRHOEA

Gonorrhoea is quite rare – with an estimated less than one in 1,000 people in the UK having it, but it is on the rise, particularly amongst gay males. Like chlamydia, it can be treated with antibiotics and it is easily tested for by a GP or at a clinic.

## HIV

**Human immunodeficiency virus (HIV)** tends not to show symptoms at first, other than early on when it often presents as a flu-like illness within a few weeks of infection that will in all likelihood be passed off as a simple cold virus. Around seventeen per cent of those who have HIV are unaware of their infection, and so at risk of unknowingly passing it on to a sexual partner. There is no cure for HIV/AIDS, but if it is found early it can be treated by antiretroviral therapy effectively. The longer it is left, the less effective the treatment. Around two in 1,000 people in the UK are living with HIV and it predominantly affects gay men and those of African ethnicity.

## HPV

HPV is a group of viruses, some of which cause genital warts, and some types can result in cervical cancer, though for most people the virus will go away on its own within a year, without causing serious health problems. Since the introduction of the highly effective HPV vaccine, which is now given to girls aged twelve to thirteen, the likelihood of girls and young women contracting HPV has now been significantly reduced. Before the vaccination programme, around one in six women had a high risk of developing HPV, and in young women the risk was higher, with a quarter of women aged eighteen to twenty-four developing it.

## PUBIC LICE

Pubic lice have nothing to do with poor hygiene. They are tiny parasitic insects that live in coarse body hair, such as pubic hair, but not in the hair on your head. They are yellow-grey in colour, about 2mm long and have a crab-like appearance, hence the common term for them of 'crabs'. Symptoms range from itching in affected areas, black powdery droppings in your underwear, brownish eggs in pubic or other body hair and either tiny sky-blue spots or blood spots on the skin. A sexual health clinic or your GP can easily diagnose pubic lice.

## SYPHILIS

Syphilis is a chronic bacterial disease that is contracted chiefly by infection during sex and is relatively rare amongst STIs. Symptoms of syphilis can include: mouth sores, usually within two to three weeks after contracting the disease; and sores on the body – but mainly on the vulva (the lips around the opening to the vagina), the clitoris, the cervix and around the opening to the urethra (the opening to the urinary tract) and the anus.

## CYSTITIS

Cystitis is not an STI, but sex can trigger it. It is usually caused by bacteria irritating the bladder lining and a common symptom is pain when you wee.

# WHAT DO YOU KNOW ABOUT PRIVATE PARTS?

Don't know about you, but I couldn't label *every* part of my vulva. So I thought we could all take the test!

Have a go at labelling below what you think the parts are . . .

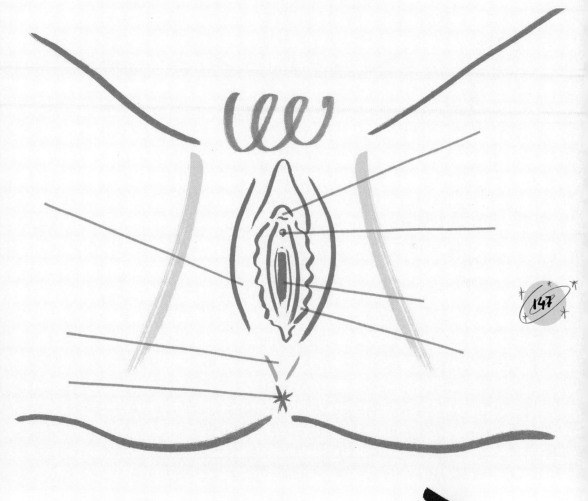

147

Turn page over to see the same picture with the correct parts labelled.

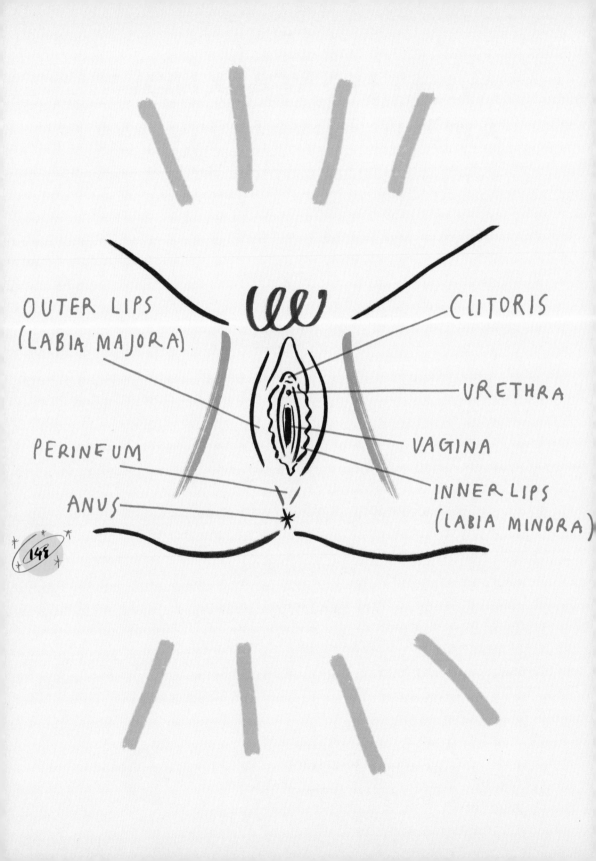

OUTER LIPS
(LABIA MAJORA)

CLITORIS

URETHRA

PERINEUM

VAGINA

ANUS

INNER LIPS
(LABIA MINORA)

148

# MASTURBATION

This is one of the most private, private things you can do, if you choose to, alone.

No one talks about it, but lots of people do it. It may be a little bit of a secret, but it's not a bad one. If you touch yourself for pleasure, it ain't nothing to be ashamed of: you are normal.

It's different strokes for different folks; everyone has their own way of doing it.

You are allowed to be inquisitive about sex and have fantasies.

Masturbation WILL NOT make you pregnant or ill.

It is not, I repeat NOT, bad for your health.

## Thank goodnesssssssss!

# 1. You cannot unsee things

It is important, if you decide to access porn, to make sure you don't upset yourself by being led down the wrong path. There's an incredibly foggy land of porn out there, and just because it is accessible doesn't mean it is right for us all to view. The wrong kind of porn or too much porn can affect our real lives when it goes beyond fantasy, and it can lead to both addiction and intimacy issues. Trust your gut – if you feel like something isn't quite right in some way or disturbs you, never forget that the power of the OFF button is yours. And never forget the power of your own imagination alone when it comes to sexual fantasy. It's within your control, and it is so much better.

# 2. It is unrealistic

The positions, the bodies, the scenarios, the pleasure portrayed in porn is not true to real life. Real sex is messier, hairier, more awkward and therefore way more fun! Real sex usually involves two people who either really love or fancy each other. There are all sorts of emotions and noises to discover that are not represented in porn. In porn, it's an actor's job to pretend and to fit into a hyper-sexualized context, because the porn industry makes major bucks that way, not because the porn stars know something we don't. If you are going to watch it, then that's your choice. Don't demonize yourself . . . but DO protect yourself by knowing that it's worlds away from what it's really like to have sex. You can't expect real-life sex to represent anything you see in porn.

151

# 3. It is possible to get addicted

It is very easy to get addicted to the short, sharp hit porn can give you. As with everything we do, moderation is key. Always assess whether it's making you feel bad or guilty, or whether you can't get it off your mind.

If you are worried that someone you know is too into porn, and it's affecting them, speak to them calmly and explain your concerns. Even if it's embarrassing. They may not realize that it's the porn that is affecting their behaviour.

Please refer to organizations at the back of this book for extra help on porn addiction and educating ourselves on the porn phenomenon.

# CONSENT, RAPE AND RAPE CULTURE

In the eyes of the law, if someone doesn't consent to a sexual act, then it's a criminal offence to have sex with them. No grey area: if one person doesn't want to do it, IT SHOULDN'T HAPPEN. And if you are under sixteen, and have felt intimidated into saying yes, or not saying no, to sex – but did not want it to happen – it is rape.

This is regardless of how intoxicated someone might be, regardless of what someone might be wearing, regardless of what's happened up until the moment they decide they don't want to. I know lots of girls and women live with a fear of sexual violence lurking in the shadows, for the simple reason that men are physically stronger. This DOES NOT mean that it doesn't happen to men too, though.

Consent, rape and rape culture are the most complex issues I've ever had to cover on the Radio 1 *Surgery* show. It's so important that we all know what rape is, and what to do if it happens to us or one of our friends. It is too important to ignore. It is a taboo subject, and that's because it's a hard and scary subject. But that doesn't mean we shouldn't talk about it.

I spoke to a brave and inspiring young woman who had been a victim of sexual violence about what she wishes she had more information about when it happened to her. The following interview contains descriptions of an upsetting and graphic nature, and may be triggering if you've experienced sexual violence. If you want to skip it, that's OK.

**GC:** Do you consider yourself a victim? Is it something that kind of forms part of you?

**A:** I think that was one of the biggest things that bothered me afterwards in terms of all the literature you get given, and every system that you have to go through for various aspects. They always refer to you as 'victim'. Again, from my personal experience, that just brings out the loss of control and power over your own body and over your own being. In my view, it basically gives that little bit more, again, to both the perpetrator and also to other people, which, following something like rape, is the last thing that you want.

You read these pamphlets and booklets, everything you get given, but no one knows exactly how someone is going to react. There are moments that are like riding a rollercoaster, at least at first it was very much about trying not to think about it. After weeks I'd wake up and I'd be able to get up and brush my teeth, and I wouldn't have thought about it until then. Those periods get longer and longer, until you make it through an entire morning.

There are times when I can make it through two days, but, there's always the potential for something to trigger it back. And it can be the most innocuous, tiniest little thing that has happened before and hasn't triggered it, but for whatever reason, it does [this time], and it just brings you right back. That can happen at any point.

I was at a work event last November — it was a fancy-dress party thing — I had a glass of Prosecco, and I went to drop off my empty glass, and . . . I smelt the same aftershave that the person that raped me had been wearing. It's a very common aftershave — you smell it on the tube, you smell it in the office, you smell it in shops, pubs, everywhere — but, for whatever reason, that just brought me right back straight away. It's little things like that. I don't think it's something that you can ever truly get over while there are still triggers that will still bring you straight back.

**GC:** Why do you think it's important for people to report sexual abuse, assault and violence of all forms?

**A:** I think, for me, the biggest thing was that I don't think I could've lived with myself if I found out that he'd done the same thing to someone else. I didn't want that guilt and that burden and that worry. I think, as hard as going through a case is, the outcome, in the sense that — not that I'd done my bit, or even that I'd stopped them doing it again — it is a weight off my mind in terms of I haven't got that constant fear of a knock on the door or a call from someone at the Met Sapphire unit . . . to ask me the question, 'Do [you] want to pursue it now?' It's done and dusted. I think the fact that I know that he's off the streets is good . . . There is no sentence that could've been passed down by the courts that would ever make up for what happened to me. I've got something that will affect me for the rest of my life, and it makes certain aspects of my life very difficult — relationships, trusting people . . .

**GC:** What about all the stuff that's in the news about people that don't get sentenced properly?

**A:** I don't think it's a perfect system. I also don't think that just locking someone up for twenty years is going to cause any real good in the long run. I think there needs to be a lot more in terms of rehabilitation of offenders. People coming in and out of prison is just getting bigger and bigger, and it's almost a self-fulfilling prophecy in the fact that it then means there's less resources to help rehabilitation, which then just makes the problem worse because you get more people going back in.

**GC:** Would you have any advice for people that know someone who has experienced sexual violence, in terms of how they should speak to them about it, or if they should at all?

**A:** Just be there. I told my best friend, and she came round and she brought a bottle of wine and some kind of fizzy grape juice — non-alcoholic thing — because she wasn't sure if I'd want to drink or not, and she brought some ice cream and some fruit, because she wasn't sure if I wanted to eat junk food or eat fruit. She tried to cover all bases, and it actually injected a little bit of humour into the situation . . . Yeah, it was just — it was being there. And we started watching *Ab Fab* or something, and then I did start to open up and talk a little bit. She was just there to . . . listen. I'd probably say don't ask questions . . . Just be there to listen and just digest what they say.

**GC:** Has there been any organization, or online portal, or support group that you would recommend that has been particularly helpful?

**A:** As soon as possible after it happens, I would highly recommend the Havens — these are centres across London (other similar organizations exist around the country) — they're completely anonymous and basically you can get forensics taken that are then stored, that then if you wanted to pursue a case later on, you do have that option available, which, if you don't do that, it can make things incredibly difficult. They in no way put any pressure on you to report it, or not report it — they just store this on file. And they can also, if you want them to for forensic purposes, store your clothing.

They also can arrange counselling if you want. They have on-site counsellors. I know that you can do that through them, and they're a service that will assist you for the first year.

They have got a proper dedicated medical team, and in my case my rape was quite violent, and they were able to deal with my other medical needs at the time as well, which meant that I didn't have to go through A&E or anything, which . . . just that kind of peace and quiet was very helpful, and also not having to see various different doctors and nurses, just kind of be looked after by one doctor and a nurse was helpful for me.

**GC:** Societally, do you feel like there needs to be a shift in our attitude towards rape?

**A:** I definitely became more in tune with certain things . . . There are an awful lot of jokes that are made about rape that I think we're almost used to because of similar 'banter' — it's like we've almost tuned out of how awful they are, because we do hear them quite a lot . . .

As a society we seem to think it's OK to joke about that kind of thing. The one that always gets me every time is, 'It's not rape if you shout "surprise".'

As far as I'm concerned, there is no grey area, there are no blurred lines: someone either consents to sex or they don't. There is no grey area or miscommunication. I don't care how many drinks or dinners or whatever you've bought someone, and I don't care if they've happily gone up to your flat, or invited you in and got into bed and are halfway through — as soon as they turn around and say no, that means no.

**GC:** **What about advice for those in a relationship with someone who has experienced sexual violence or assault – what would you say?**

**A:** Relationships are difficult. There's going to be a whole range of emotions. With me, there was a complete lack of trust . . . I really wanted to open up and trust, and I found it incredibly difficult. I think just be there, again, listen, be guided by the other person. As human beings, we're almost pre-designed to be selfish and self-centred and think everything is because of something we've done. This is certainly much bigger than that. Just because something was fine last week, don't assume it's going to be fine this week. It took me the best part of three years to even get into a position where I was prepared to have a relationship with somebody, and I still find sex very difficult. Again, there is support out there. There are groups that meet, and you can decide whether you want to discuss various things. I know a lot of people have got a lot of help from that.

159

My Body Back is a project that specializes in supporting those who've experienced sexual violence and assault. Their site features an in-depth list of their services, and a clear list of the different charities dealing with various related issues, regardless of where you are in the UK, or what your particular experience is – from LGBTQ specialists to prevention of forced arranged marriages.

**Head to www.mybodybackproject.com**

There are also more organizations listed at the back of the book that can help.

# FINALLY

Be gentle and patient with yourself and give yourself the time to work out the inner rhythms of your body and soul, whether it's the *boom, boom* of a loud giant drum, or a rain-like patter on a bongo. As you evolve and grow, these rhythms will become more layered, like an orchestra. It takes time to feel comfortable with that, and to learn to accept it: stay OPEN and your journey to understanding your individual body and soul can be as exhilarating as it is exhausting.

# USEFUL WEBSITES

## YOUR HEART

**Abusive Relationships**
www.lovedontfeelbad.co.uk
www.womensaid.org.uk

**Emotional and Physical Abuse (Teens)**
www.childline.org.uk
www.nspcc.org.uk

**Bullying**
www.ditchthelabel.org
www.bulliesout.com
www.kidscape.org.uk
www.antibullyingpro.com

**Loneliness**
www.mind.org.uk/Loneliness

**Bereavement**
www.winstonswish.org.uk
www.rainbowtrust.org.uk
www.muchloved.com
www.cruse.org.uk

## YOUR BODY AND SOUL

**Body Image**
www.bodycharity.co.uk
www.berealcampaign.co.uk
www.bodygossip.org

**Periods**
www.periodpositive.com

**Rape and Sexual Offences**
content.met.police.uk/Site/sapphire
www.mybodybackproject.com
www.rapecrisis.org.uk
www.thesurvivorstrust.org

**Asexuality**
www.whatisasexuality.com

**LGBTQ Charities**
www.akt.org.uk
www.stonewall.org.uk
www.glaad.org
www.itgetsbetter.org

**Transgender Charities/Organizations**
www.genderedintelligence.co.uk
www.mermaidsuk.org.uk

**Sexual Health**
whenitsonitson.durex.co.uk
www.brook.org.uk
www.fpa.org.uk

**Abortion**
www.bpas.org
www.mariestopes.org.uk
www.nupas.co.uk

**Porn**
www.porn-recovery.co.uk
www.cosrt.org.uk
www.sexaddictionhelp.co.uk
www.atsac.co.uk

# THANK YOU!

A thanks and a big-up to Paradise Apartments and Alex's Bar in Sarakiniko, for putting up with me meandering around the gaff like a crazed pup with computers for eyes and leaving me to it, typing like a nut in apartment No. 9. A time never to be forgotten, days before the EU Referendum vote; the internet turning me sometimes into a sobbing mess.

Thank you, Mrs Dragon, for your perfect combination of warm and smiley wicked giggles. Plus little Riko too, for merely providing the brilliance and innocence of a baby genius who loves the sea even more than I do.

Thank you to Sara Jane at the Coach House, for providing the perfect solitary escape.

Thank you, Becky Thomas, for listening to my hare-brained idea, when I collared you in a stinky pub. Thank you, Rachel P and Gaby, for reining me in. Thank you, Emily, for being my carer. Thank you, Rachel V, for not writing swear words back when I was being so clueless and yet bossy in my emails. Thank you, Kat, for sharing the wheels-on-the-bus-going-round-and-round vision from the get-go. Thank you to Bea, for your lovely energy of enthusiasm and care for this project! Thank you to all of team *Open*. YOU are AMAZING.

Thank you, Aurelia. WOW you have blown us away. Anyone who takes a manic message about a smiling condom and makes it into an iconic picture is frankly magnificent.

Thank you, SJ, for being the slickest and most resilient life cheerleader always.

Thank you, Woo, for ALWAYS feeding and challenging my brain, and for listening to me relentlessly wang ON.

Thank you, BriGaz, you are a treasure to know – and give endless inspiration and love.

Thank you to ALL ma crew. My friends for always nodding when I'm chatting tripe, scooping me up when I go crazy, never making me feel judged or misunderstood, for being the BEST FUN. YEP, that's you, brother from another mother and deep inspiration Laurence (aka Lozini); you, my forever bestie Camilla (CamCam); Scott (Scottie-too-hottie); beautiful and kind Sarah (Baker), Sam (aka monsieur le mayor) and your new addition baby Bow; Dallanda (aka Trojan), gorgeous Niklas and your magic Baby Issaga; determined and brilliant Claudia (Cloudini) and Matt (Clark Kent), thank you for always supporting me in the *Birmingham Mail*. Thank you, Amy (Zing), for being as warm and colourful as a walking rainbow and introducing me to a home town I could find the calm to write a book in.

Thank you to Katie V, for trawling through lots of gabbing.

Thanks, Amber and Rob, for not batting an eyelid when I was a sweaty monster furiously typing in my room and regurgitating angst during the process.

Thank you, to the boyz, the loves of the past mentioned in *Open*, for you have helped to teach me lots of what I am – how to love, heal and love again. Thank you, Mr Smith.

Thank you to Becky and Daniella, the most patient and talented videographers in the country.

Thank you, Nash and Dockers, for being gifted, wordy dreamers and for making feel like I could be the same.

Thank you to all those at the Beeb, who trained me up good and proper, and believed in me to give the opportunities that you have.

Thank you to those in my industry who I count as dear and supportive friends and mad-core inspirationals – that's you, Lala & Dawn.

Thank you to Mum, Laura and Daddy Cool for continuously putting up with me.

AND OF COURSE ALL THE CONTRIBUTORSSSSS . . . You were too ace for me not to include you in this book.

AURELIA LANGE >
ILLUSTRATOR

LAURA CAIRNEY-KEIZE >
PAGE 93

LAUREN > PAGE 13

ANNA HART >
PAGE 92

AMY REDMOND >
PAGE 93

JESSICA JORDAN-WRENCH > PAGE 92
© KIM CONWAY

GEORGE LESTER >
EDITORIAL ASSISTANT

GEORGIA LEWIS-ANDERSON
> PAGE 93

JUNO DAWSON > PAGE 127
© JOEL RIDER

ZEZI IFORE > PAGE 92

MARAWA CAMARA >
PAGE 71

LEO PEMBERTON >
PAGE 114

KAT MCKENNA >
MARKETING MANAGER

LITERARY AGENT >
BECKY THOMAS

DR RADHA > PAGE 83

BEA CROSS >
PUBLICITY MANAGER

JESSICA THANDI BERRY >
PAGE 93

NIC ADDISON > PAGE 108

EMMA GIBSON > PAGE 92
© GABRIELLE HALL

SOPHIE AND OSCAR > PAGE 13

JANENE SPENCER >
DESIGNER

ANONYMOUS
INTERVIEW >
PAGE 154

EMILY THOMAS > EDITOR

BRIGITTE APHRODITE > PAGES
19 + 92
© OLIVIER RICHOMME

MICHAEL > PAGE 13

GEORGIE OKELL > PAGE 121
© JON LAWTON

RACHEL VALE >
ART DIRECTOR

PROF HUGH MONTGOMERY
> PAGE 65

EDITORIAL DIRECTOR
NON-FICTION & POETRY
> GABY MORGAN

SURAN D AND SONNY > PAGE 124

KELLY ABBOT > PAGE 138

FRANCES ACQUAAH >
PAGES 52 + 93

RACHEL PETTY > EDITORIAL
DIRECTOR

KATIE V > TRANSCRIBING WHIZZ

SUSIE ORBACH > PAGE 88

# INDEX